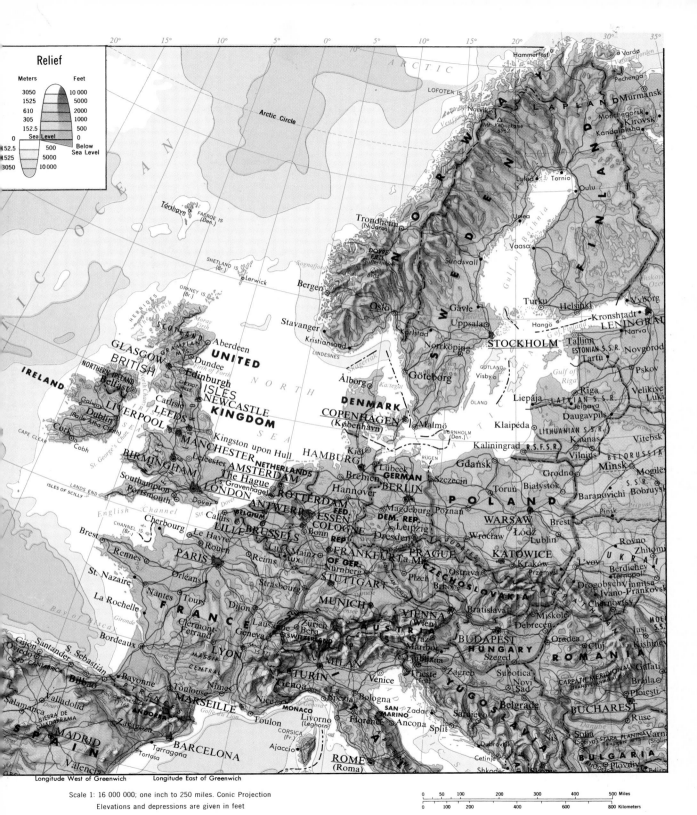

Relief

Meters		Feet
3050		10 000
1525		5000
610		2000
305		1000
152.5		500
0	Sea Level	0
152.5		500
1525		5000
3050	Below Sea Level	10 000

ARCTIC OCEAN

Arctic Circle

ATLANTIC OCEAN

Tórshavn FAERØE IS. (Den.)

SHETLAND IS. (Br.) Lerwick

ORKNEY IS. (Br.)

HEBRIDES

NORTH SEA

IRELAND

Galway Dublin Baile Átha Cliath

Cork Cobh

CAPE CLEAR

ISLES OF SCILLY LANDS END

GLASGOW BRITISH
NORTHERN IRELAND Belfast
SCOTLAND
GRAMPIAN MTS. Aberdeen
Dundee
Edinburgh UNITED
Carlisle CHEVIOT HILLS ISLES
NEWCASTLE KINGDOM
LIVERPOOL LEEDS
Kingston upon Hull
MANCHESTER
BIRMINGHAM Leicester NETHERLANDS AMSTERDAM
Southampton The Hague 's Gravenhage
Portsmouth LONDON ROTTERDAM
Dover ANTWERP
English Channel Str. of Dover Calais BELGIUM BRUSSELS
Cherbourg Le Havre LILLE ESSEN
CHANNEL IS. (Br.) Rouen COLOGNE
Brest Reims Lux. Mainz BONN
Rennes PARIS Nürnberg FRANKFURT a. M.
St. Nazaire Orléans STUTTGART
Nantes Tours Dijon
La Rochelle Strasbourg
FRANCE Clermont-Ferrand Lausanne Zürich MUNICH
Bordeaux Geneva Bern SWITZERLAND
LYON Mont Blanc VIENNA (Wien)
Bayonne MASSIF TURIN MILAN
Toulouse CENTRAL Genoa Venice
PYRENEES Nice La Spezia Bologna
Santander S. Sebastián MARSEILLE MONACO Florence
Gijón Bilbao SIERRA DE GUADARRAMA ANDORRA CORSICA (Fr.) Livorno (Leghorn) SAN MARINO Ancona
Oviedo Valladolid Toulon Ajaccio
Salamanca Zaragoza BARCELONA ROME (Roma)
MADRID Tarragona
SPAIN Tortosa
Valencia

Hammerfest Vardø

LOFOTEN IS. Narvik LAPLAND Murmansk
Pechenga Monchegorsk Kirovsk
Kandalaksha
NORWAY Kebnekaise 6982
Luleå Tornio
SWEDEN Oulu
Trondheim (Nidaros) Umeå Vaasa
DOVRE FJELL Sundsvall FINLAND
Bergen Gävle Turku Helsinki Vyborg
Oslo Uppsala Hangö Kronshtadt
Stavanger Norrköping STOCKHOLM LENINGRAD
Kristiansand GOTLAND Tallinn Narva
Göteborg Visby ESTONIAN S.S.R. Novgorod
Ålborg ÖLAND Tartu
DENMARK Liepāja LATVIAN S.S.R. Pskov
COPENHAGEN (København) Malmö Riga Velikiye Luki
BORNHOLM (Den.) Klaipėda Jelgava
HAMBURG RÜGEN Kaliningrad R.S.F.S.R. Daugavpils
Kiel Lübeck Gdańsk Kaunas LITHUANIAN S.S.R. Vitebsk
Bremen GERMAN BERLIN Szczecin Vilnius
AMSTERDAM Hannover Grodno Minsk
FED. Magdeburg Poznań POLAND Białystok BELORUSSIA Mogilëv
DEM. REP. Leipzig Baranovichi Bobruysk
REP. Dresden WARSAW S.S.R.
OF GER. Bonn Wrocław Łódź Brest Pinsk
Leipzig Lublin
Ostrava Kraków Rovno Zhitomir
PRAGUE KATOWICE Przemyśl L'vov UKRAINE
CZECHOSLOVAKIA Plzeň Brno Berdichev
Drogobych Ternopol
Bratislava Miskolc Ivano-Frankovsk
Graz Debrecen Chernovtsy MOL. S.S.R.
Maribor HUNGARY Oradea Jassy
Ljubljana BUDAPEST Szeged Cluj ROMANIA
Zagreb Subotica Kishinev
Trieste Novi Sad Galați
Venice Zadar YUGOSLAVIA Braila
Sarajevo Belgrade Ploiești
Split BUCHAREST Ruse
Dubrovnik Niš Danube STARA PLANINA Varna
Cetinje Sofia (Sofiya) BULGARIA
Shkodër Plovdiv

Longitude West of Greenwich   Longitude East of Greenwich

Scale 1: 16 000 000; one inch to 250 miles. Conic Projection

Elevations and depressions are given in feet

0	50	100	200	300	400	500 Miles
0	100	200	400	600	800 Kilometers	

© Copyright by Rand McNally & Co. R.L. 86-S-44

Enchantment of the World

SWITZERLAND

By Martin Hintz

Consultants for Switzerland: Jean Devaud, M.S., Professor Emeritus, City Colleges of Chicago, Illinois; Marie-Simone Pavlovich, Ph.D., Northwestern University, Evanston, Illinois

Consultant for Reading: Robert L. Hillerich, Ph.D., Bowling Green State University, Bowling Green, Ohio

CHILDRENS PRESS®
CHICAGO

The Castle of Chillon

To my Kate, who can hurdle mountains with her heart

Library of Congress Cataloging-in-Publication Data

Hintz, Martin.
  Switzerland.

  (Enchantment of the world)
  Includes index.
  Summary: An introduction to the geography, history,
economy, famous sites, people, and cultures of the
humanitarian nation that is only twice as large as Minnesota.
    1.   Switzerland—Juvenile literature.
[1.   Switzerland]   I.   Title.   II.   Series.
DQ17.H53   1986   949.4   86-9581
ISBN 0-516-02790-5

Picture Acknowledgments
Image Finders: © Lu Hamacek, 4, 58 (left), 67 (top), 80
Root Resources: © Rosel Roth, 5, 86 (bottom left), 94;
© Barbara Adams, 17; © Jana R. Jirak, 23 (right); © Kenneth
Rapalee, 57 (right); © Russel A. Kriete, 73, 111 (left)
Valan Photos: © Val & Alan Wilkinson, 8, 84; © Denis Roy,
86 (bottom right); © Jean-Marie Jro, 110 (top left)
Nawrocki Stock Photo: © Wm. S. Nawrocki, 82; © D.J.
Variakojis, 9 (left), 14, 19, 21 (left), 36, 51 (right), 54 (left),
57 (left), 60, 61 (2 photos), 62 (2 photos), 63 (2 photos), 64
(top right & left, bottom left), 69 (2 photos), 70 (right), 74
(right), 75, 95, 97 (left), 107; © Mark Stevenson, 9 (right),
70 (left); © Ted Cordingley, 74 (left), 92 (left)
Bob & Ira Spring: 13, 15 (left), 23 (left), 79 (right), 111
(right), 113
© **M.B. Rosalsky:** 10 (bottom)
© **H. Armstrong Roberts, Inc:** Cover, 10 (top), 38, 40, 52,
66, 78 (2 photos), 81
© **H. Armstrong Roberts/Camerique:** 6, 79 (left)
© **Mary Ann Brockman:** 15 (right), 24 (bottom), 48 (top),
86 (top left)
Tom Stack & Associates: © Leonard Lee Rue III, 21 (right);
© Brian Parker, 22 (left)
Photri: 22 (right), 55 (left), 110 (top right), 112
Associated Press: 24 (top)
The Granger Collection: 27
EKM-Nepenthe: © Thomas Coard, 28, 48 (bottom), 86
(center right), 91, 105 (left); © Peter Tartsanyi, 55 (right)
Historical Pictures Service, Chicago: 30 (left), 44
(2 photos), 92 (right), 105 (right)
© **Virginia Grimes:** 30 (right)
Swiss National Tourist Office: 34, 51 (left), 53 (right), 97
(right), 101 (left), 108 (right), 109 (2 photos)
Journalism Services: © Dave Brown, 53 (left), 101 (right),
102 (left), 104, 108 (left); © Dirk Gallian, 64 (bottom right);
© Harry J. Przekop, Jr., 85
Worldwide Photo: 54 (right), 58 (right), 59, 83, 86 (top
right)
© **Chandler Forman:** 67 (bottom)
© **Tony Freeman:** 98
© **Art Resource,** 102 (right)
Maps by Len Meents: 33, 49, 107
Courtesy Flag Research Center, Winchester,
Massachusetts 01890: Flag on back cover
Cover: Switzerland in winter

A farmer from the Toggenburg Valley carries cowbells used for cattle drives.

TABLE OF CONTENTS

Chapter 1

COMPACT, CLEAN,
AND CHARITABLE

Switzerland is rich in scenery, a jumble of cloud-spearing mountains on a chessboard of fields, forests, and booming cities. It is a compact country, nestled into an area about half the size of Indiana or Maine.

It is not only a land of yodeling, watchmaking, downhill skiing, and fine chocolate. Delightful as they may be, there is much more to this enchanting land. Its people are the key to what makes Switzerland the enjoyable place it is. Adventurous, artistic, and industrious, they have a broad, eager outlook on life.

As one of the world's major financial centers, Switzerland caters to Middle Eastern sheiks, Western industrialists, Hollywood movie stars, as well as day-to-day tourists. Switzerland is also a gracious host to multinational conferences that debate arms control, discuss drought prevention, or argue over crude-oil prices. It is a leading humanitarian nation, straightforward in its political neutrality and outgoing with its technical, charitable, and economic largesse.

Switzerland is famous for wood carvings and chalets. It also is highly industrialized, overflowing with engineering genius and a capability to manufacture goods ranging from monstrous turbines to intricate, tiny timepieces.

Opposite page: The Bernese Alps

A Swiss chalet

Even with its factories, there is nothing grimy about
Switzerland. Electrical power and lots of old-fashioned elbow
grease on the part of its people keep the atmosphere and
countryside clean, neat, and fresh.

As one of the oldest democracies in the world, Switzerland has
long been a leading advocate of peace, justice, and international
cooperation. Although Switzerland is dwarfed geographically by
most other nations, its prestige as a mediator far outweighs its
size.

Swiss citizens can be found throughout the world, as medical
personnel, technical advisers, diplomats, and in many other
professions that advance the welfare of others.

Accommodating, gracious, delightful—the Swiss are that and
more. However, as with any large family, they sometimes argue
among themselves as to the proper qualities of the "best" Swiss.
Residents of Zürich mutter about the "thickheaded" citizens of

German is the predominant language spoken by citizens of Basel (left) and Zürich (right).

Basel. Basel citizens joke about the "dour sensibilities" of the Zürichers.

A French-speaking Swiss from the west might never admit to liking a German-speaking Swiss from the north—and vice versa. Every hamlet is fiercely independent and proud of its identity. Early in Swiss history, such parochial attitudes occasionally plunged the countryside into civil war.

Today, the bantering is simply friendly needling. Each Swiss considers it proper to gently tease other citizens. But don't let an outsider try the same thing. That's when the Swiss forget their perceived differences. They band together and confront any attacking outsider. In the old days, invading armies quickly learned not to tangle with the combined ferocity of the Swiss. It is obvious, therefore, that behind the jokes is a definite all-encompassing love of homeland.

Switzerland's impressive mountain peaks, such as
the Jungfrau (above right) at 14,295 feet (4,357 meters) and Dent
Blanche (below) reaching 13,640 (4,158 meters), are surrounded
by beautiful scenery.

Chapter 2

LAND OF MOUNTAINS

Finding one word to describe Swiss topography is easy. The entire geographical story is summed up by *solid*. This is obvious on the observation platform atop the Kleine (Little) Matterhorn near Zermatt. Twenty-nine of the thirty-eight peaks in Switzerland that are higher than thirteen thousand feet (about four thousand meters) are in view. The famous Matterhorn can be seen jabbing the blue sky with its needle-nosed peak towering 14,692 feet (4,478 meters). That dangerous-to-climb massif, or central portion of a mountain, is flanked by the Dent d'Herens, Dent Blanche, Mount Duran, and a dozen other lofty craigs. The list of rock continues: the Weisshorn, the Täschhorn, Monte Rosa, and more. *Solid*, all of them.

Switzerland's jumbled peaks seem to roll on forever. Switzerland's highest point, Dufourspitze (Dufour Peak) of the Monte Rosa group at 15,204 feet (4,634 meters), probably appears no different today than it did during the last Ice Age twenty thousand years ago.

FORMATION OF THE MOUNTAINS

However, 130 million years ago, there were no mountains in what is now Switzerland. The entire country was covered by an ancient body of water called the Tethys Sea. On the bottom of this sea was mud and other sediment. As the earth moved and groaned beneath, the sediment and rock was pushed around. Over thousands of years, huge plates of earth slid back and forth. At the edges of the plates, molten lava bubbled forth and was cooled in that expansive body of water.

Bit by bit, eighty million years ago, solid rock was pushed above the water to become the tips of today's mountains. Forty million years ago, more land was visible. Fifteen million years ago, the sea had disappeared and the earth's crust hardened. About five million years ago, the earth heaved again and pushed the mountains even higher.

Geologists can tell what changes occurred during that violent period by studying the layers of limestone exposed on the cliff faces.

THE MOVING WALLS OF ICE

The rough chiseling effect of wind, rain, and snow is still shaping the Alps, the name given to the Swiss mountain system. Primary among the mountain sculptors are glaciers, which stretch through many of the folds in the high Alps. They are shifting, moving rivers of ice and snow hundreds of feet high, pushing tons of rocks and debris ahead of them. The glaciers are formed by ice and snow compacted into a very dense mass that moves forward by the pressure of its weight.

For a closer look at these moving walls of ice, sightseers can walk through tunnels carved in the glaciers. One excellent trip is a winter's stroll through the Rhone glacier in the canton (state) of Valais. A boardwalk through the heart of the frozen river takes visitors into an eerie world of blue-green ice.

Aletsch glacier, the longest glacier in Switzerland ‹

The glaciers are only vestiges of the enormous sea of ice that almost covered the mountains during the Ice Age. Currently, they cover 601 square miles (1,556 square kilometers). The Aletsch glacier in Valais is the longest in Europe, measuring 15 miles (24 kilometers) in length.

GEOGRAPHIC DIVISIONS

The Alps are the largest mountain system in Europe. They extend over France, northern Italy, Switzerland, Liechtenstein, southern West Germany, Austria, and northern Yugoslavia.

Switzerland is divided into three geographical sections: the Swiss Alps, the Jura Mountains, and the plateau (or Mittelland). The Swiss Alps make up the southern frontier with Italy. The jagged peaks of the Jura Mountains spread from west to northeast along the border with France. Several glaciers crawl out of these ranges, inching down through steep mountain passes.

Farmlands near Langnau in central Switzerland

The heart of the country is the broad, fertile plateau, where about two thirds of the population lives. This rolling tableland stretches from Genève through Luzern and on into Germany.

The plateau is crisscrossed by electric railways, highways, and sparkling rivers such as the Rhone and the Limmat. It is Switzerland's breadbasket as well as its industrial center.

In addition to France and Italy, landlocked Switzerland's other neighbors include Germany on the north and Austria and Liechtenstein on the east.

THE MAJESTIC MOUNTAINS

The mountains can be dangerous. Barricades and protective walls line many of the steeper slopes in an effort to deflect or halt landslides. Sometimes the plan works, sometimes it doesn't. Even the cities in the plateau are affected by the Alps. Flash flooding of the mountain streams can cause much damage, even with dikes and dams, as the rushing water roars out of the gorges.

The majestic Alps, which cover about 60 percent of the Swiss landscape, received their name from the early Romans. Scholars believe that *Alp* evolved from the Latin word *alb*, which means

Between the mountain peaks are rushing rivers and quiet valleys.

"white," the color of the dazzling snow. *Alp* has also come to mean a high pasture where sheep and cows graze in the summer.

Twenty percent of the 650-mile (1,046-kilometer) long chain of Alps is in Switzerland. Valleys divide the links into distinct sections. The northeastern ranges are called the Glarner, Schwyzer, and Eastern Urner Alps; the northwestern portions are the Western Urner, Unterwaldner, Bernese, Fribourg, and Vaud Alps; the southern Alps are the Valais, Ticino, and Grisons Alps.

However, the Alps aren't the only Swiss pinnacles. The fossil-rich Jura Mountains, with their lush meadows and thick forest cover, spread over 10 percent of the countryside, primarily in northwestern Switzerland abutting France. These older mountains are more weather-beaten and worn than the Alps. The Jura peaks average 2,450 feet (750 meters) high, compared to the average Alpine height of 3,550 feet (1,082 meters). They have given their name to the Jurassic period of history 136 million years ago.

DISTANCES DOWN AND ACROSS

Yet not all of Switzerland is precariously perched atop a mountain ledge. Switzerland shares its lowest point, Lake Maggiore, 633 feet (193 meters) above sea level, with its southern neighbor, Italy. Three quarters of the population lives in the heart of lowland Switzerland, with its cities, rivers, and orchards. In addition, most of the country's major industries are located here as well, peeking out from the gentle rolling fields.

Switzerland is small, only 15,942 square miles (41,288 square kilometers). From north to south, the maximum distance is 138 miles (222 kilometers); from east to west, the greatest distance is 213 miles (343 kilometers). The length of the Swiss frontier is 1,169 miles (1,881 kilometers).

PEAKS TO SCALE

No matter where a traveler goes in Switzerland, the presence of the mountains can always be felt. Certainly, the mountains have been divisive by isolating pockets of Swiss in the days when travel was difficult. Yet they have also created fiercely independent people, who rely on their own wits and ingenuity. Indeed, the mountains are also protection, preventing modern invaders from conquering the interior of this natural fortress.

Yet as late as the mid-1800s, visitors to Switzerland were afraid of the desertlike cliffs devoid of vegetation, scoured by wind, and slammed by harsh changes in temperature. Few people attempted any mountain climbing for scientific research, much less for fun.

The adventurous English were among the first to scale the peaks. Looking for vacation excitement and an escape from the

Climbing the Matterhorn can be dangerous, but it is thrilling.

humdrum life of the cities, they flocked to Switzerland in the 1850s and 1860s. The adventurers were intent on challenging and defeating the grim mountains. Switzerland became Europe's playground during those "Golden Years" of Alpine climbing. But the excursions were dangerous and often deadly, even for experienced mountaineers. There is a small cemetery in Zermatt where Swiss and foreign victims who attempted to climb the sheer sides of the neighboring Matterhorn are buried.

Even when that mountain was finally conquered by a party of Englishmen, led by Edward Whymper, and their Swiss guides on July 14, 1865, the peak got its revenge. On the descent, a safety rope broke, and four of the party tumbled 4,000 feet (1,219 meters) to their death. Queen Victoria of England wanted to ban her countrymen from climbing the Matterhorn after that accident. But the thrill of climbing lured many others to take up the challenge of the Alps. The Alpine Museum in Zermatt, opened in

1904, contains hundreds of mementos of hardy climbers who risked their lives over the years. Today, guides take novice climbers to the nearby Riffelhorn, 9,606 feet (2,928 meters), for a half day of scaling rocks. This allows the guides to test the skills of anyone who wants to ascend the Matterhorn itself.

The Swiss themselves became avid mountain climbers. After all, somebody had to guide the visitors! Today, there are probably more than 30,000 active climbers in the country. One of the main climbing organizations, the Swiss Alpine Club, recently had 45,000 members on its rolls.

The impact of the peaks on the national spirit of Switzerland is summed up in a Latin inscription chiseled into a cross at the Oberalp Pass. It reads: *Ex montibus salus* ("All good comes from the mountains").

RIVERS AND LAKES

With all its snow, Switzerland has an abundance of generally clean water. The mountains are the birthplace for some of Europe's major rivers, including the Rhine and the Rhone. Water from melting glaciers eventually ends up in the Mediterranean Sea or the distant North Sea. The Aare River is the country's major water link between the lakes of Zürich and Neuchâtel. Of all these waterways, however, only the Rhine is easily navigable. Servicing ports such as Basel is a Swiss "navy," fleets of merchant vessels that ply Europe's inland waterways.

There are at least fourteen hundred pristine bodies of water scattered around Switzerland. Some were formed in kettles of rock hollowed out by retreating glaciers. Others were created behind prehistoric rockslides. Lake Geneva (Lac Léman), Lake Lucerne

The Aare River flows through the city of Bern.

(Vierwaldstättersee), and the Bodensee (which is shared with West Germany) are some of the better-known larger lakes. Ships packed with sightseers cruise the waters.

A different sort of lake is a "karst lake." It is formed when water seeps into limestone and resurfaces elsewhere. The biggest karst lake is Lac de Joux in the Jura Mountains. There are many man-made lakes as well, usually behind large power dams. The gigantic Grande Dixence Dam in the Valais, one of the highest dams in the world, forms Lac des Dix.

CLIMATE: BEST AND WORST

Because Switzerland lies in the heart of Europe, it captures the best and worst climatic conditions from all points on the compass. The lowlands, mountains, valleys, and lake regions have their peculiar weather differences. In the summer, Zürich's temperature can be as high as 86 degrees Fahrenheit (30 degrees Celsius). But it can plummet to minus 25 degrees Fahrenheit (minus 31.7 degrees Celsius) in the frosty winter. The lowlands are chilled with harsh, cold air in the winter, when a heavy mist often blots out the sunlight for days. The Swiss rise above these discomforts and travel to their mountains for skiing and other outdoor sports. Above the cloud layer, the air is often warmer and the sun bright.

The Alps form a natural division between the Mediterranean and central Europe. Moisture-filled air found in thick, heavy clouds bump headlong into the peaks and dump their rainy loads on the lowlands near the mountains. However, for centuries inland farmers have had to irrigate their fields because the rain was deposited too early in the growing season. More rain falls south of the Alps than to the north, but it falls less frequently.

From the north and east comes the cold breeze known as the *bise*, bringing frightfully frosty weather in the winter. People who live in Genève, situated in a valley between the Jura and the Alps in southwestern Switzerland, have had to get used to the *bise*. On some days, it is like living at the end of a wind tunnel.

The *föhn* is a warm southerly wind that blows out of the mountains in the early spring. The sharp turn in temperature can quickly melt snowpacks and cause thunderous avalanches. On the south side of the Alps, the air is cooler as it ascends and releases humidity, resulting in lots of rain. When it then blows down the northern slopes, the air again cools and sucks up all the moisture, almost like a desert wind. The *föhn* whistles into the valleys and stirs up the lake waters. The air is clear as crystal when the *föhn* arrives, making even distant sights appear to be nearby. As soon as the snow melts, hardy flowers carpet the landscape.

Left: Palm trees along the shore of Lake Lugano   Right: Red deer

PLANTS AND ANIMALS

The wild combination of wind, rain, and snow has contributed to an equally wide variety of plant and animal life. Mosses and lichens found in polar regions also grow in Switzerland. So do palm trees and mimosas, in the warmer climate of the canton of Ticino. Switzerland's forests consist of pines, firs, larches, beeches, and chestnut trees.

Some 11,859 square miles (30,715 square kilometers) of the country are considered productive land, suitable for crops or forestry. About one quarter of Switzerland, mostly in the high mountain areas, is unproductive.

Many wild animals still live in Switzerland's open country. Red deer are found in the southeast; roebuck are scattered throughout the country. Chamois and ibex bound from ledge to ledge in the Alps, often silhouetted against a backdrop of stone or blue sky. These cloven-hooved animals have become so numerous in some

Ibex (left) and chamois (right) live in the Alps.

parts of Switzerland that they are a nuisance. They eat the young trees and cause much crop damage.

Wild boars rummage through the cornfields of central Switzerland. Lynx, large predatory cats, lurk in the foothills. On the less fierce side, the Alpine marmot lives in the mountains. The marmot looks like a tiny, overstuffed woodchuck. It hides in large colonies amid the boulders.

The Swiss carefully protect their wildlife, demonstrating a longtime concern for animals. A magistrate named Joachim Baldi created the Karpf Game Reserve, Switzerland's first animal refuge, near Glarus in 1548. Two other protected areas are the Riegelsee Wildlife Park near Bern and the 45,000-acre (18,210-hectare) Swiss National Park, which was created in 1909 in the canton of Grisons on Italy's border. The Swiss have established fourteen botanical gardens displaying a variety of plants and eight Alpine gardens emphasizing mountain flowers.

PRESERVING THE NATURAL BEAUTY

Despite the concern shown by the Swiss, the natural growing areas for many plants have been shrinking. There is also less

The Swiss National Park is a 70-square-mile (181-square-kilometer) park in which animals and plants, such as the edelweiss (right), are protected by law.

ranging ground for wild animals. Mountain railways and footpaths have opened up the more remote regions. Some skiing enthusiasts are taken by helicopter into previously pristine areas. Naturally, this traffic disturbs the environment.

Yet many Swiss are concerned with protecting their good life. As early as 1876, the country passed a federal forestry law that safeguarded timber against overcutting. Now other projects have been started to preserve the beauty of Switzerland. The Swiss Foundation for the Protection and Care of the Landscape was formed in 1970. It coordinates the work of environmental and cultural organizations. Recently, the Swiss Society for the Protection of the Environment was chartered. Picking of certain Alpine flowers, such as the edelweiss and the great blue thistle, is strictly forbidden. Through efforts of these hardworking associations, ordinary Swiss citizens now realize that more has to be done to keep Switzerland a beautiful country.

A prehistoric village in the canton of Luzern (above) dates from about 2500 B.C. Historians believe the first permanent settlers used natural mountain passes, such as the Grimsel Pass (below), as thoroughfares.

Chapter 3

A TRADITION OF
BRAVERY

Nomadic hunters wandered into Switzerland while the monstrous ice packs of the Ice Age still ruled the harsh land. Their rudimentary weapons, household utensils, and other remains have been discovered in caves at Ebenalp (canton of Appenzell) and at Schweizerbild (canton of Schaffhausen).

Prehistoric settlers moved through the Swiss valleys in greater numbers as the ice melted away. Attracted by the protective mantle of the mountains, those ancient people found that the forests were rich with wildlife and the small fields fertile. The St. Gotthard, Bernina, and Grimsel passes through the glacier-scarred mountains were probably thoroughfares for the first permanent residents of what would become Switzerland.

During the Neolithic Stone Age, people began fashioning tools, domesticating plants and animals, and handcrafting items such as pots. For protection against attack from land, villages were built on piles driven into lake beds. This also placed the food gatherers closer to their supply of fish. Vestiges of one of these communities were first found in 1853 in Lake Zürich.

DRAGONS AND ELEPHANTS

By the Bronze Age (around 2500 B.C.), when people were learning how to use metal, tiny settlements appeared. Families usually stayed in the lowlands of the plateau, not knowing what lurked in the high meadows. Everyone "knew" there were terrible things up there. Mountain dragons and witches were blamed for throwing rocks down onto the fields. Nobody realized the rock avalanches were caused by natural forces.

The passes across the mountains not only were used by settlers, but also provided access for invaders seeking warmer climates. Roaming bands of heavily armed Celts stampeded through Switzerland, causing more damage to the hamlets and farms with swords and torches than did feared mountain dragons. By 500 B.C., one band of Celts called the Helvetii had immigrated into Switzerland in large numbers. They settled just west of the Jura Mountains and east of the Alps.

Their cultural impact has extended to contemporary times. Today's Swiss call their country *Helvetia* after these people. All official state papers, vehicle license plates, and postal codes still carry the seal of the *Confederatio Helvetica (CH)*, Swiss Confederation.

The Helvetii shared their crossroads land with another ethnic group—the Rhaeti, who migrated from northern Italy. The Rhaeti lived along the mountain passes used by the Carthaginian general Hannibal, who led an African army across the Alps to attack the Romans in the second century B.C. Hannibal's forces included some elephants, which must have created quite a stir. Scholars aren't sure, however, where Hannibal actually crossed. Some believe it was either the Mount Genèvre or Little St. Bernard pass, well-known trade routes at the time.

No one is sure how, but Hannibal and his forces did actually cross the Alps to attack the Romans.

GERMANIC TRIBES AND ROMAN LEGIONS

Warlike Germanic tribes eventually muscled their way into Helvetii territory from the north in search of a better climate. They fought their bloody way into the plateau, pushing along the easier access of the Rhone River. As the Germans moved in, the Helvetii decided to flee their homeland. In 58 B.C., thousands of them, with all their cattle and household goods, launched a massive migration west toward what is now France. The Helvetii were ready to do almost anything to get away from raids by the Germans, even to giving up their homes.

The Helvetii fled to areas that had been colonized earlier by the Romans, who weren't about to let the Helvetii settle there. Roman General Julius Caesar rushed his legions from Rome to the site of today's Genève, a distance of around five hundred miles (eight hundred kilometers). Breathless and tired after that forced march, the Roman army was still able to defeat the less organized Helvetii in a bloody battle near today's French city of Autun.

Caesar ordered the Helvetii to return to their Alpine homes, there to act as a frontier guard. The Helvetii had no choice. Back

Remains of a Roman amphitheater in Avenches,
which was an important Roman city named Aventicum

they went, accompanied by several thousand Roman soldiers to ensure their cooperation. The Romans then further extended their control over the Alps by subjugating the Rhaeti in 15 B.C.

Over the next centuries, Roman troops and governors kept order, established Roman law, and improved farming techniques. There was generally peace in the mountains and valleys until the fifth century, when Germanic tribes such as the Alemanni increased their attacks. The Romans eventually had to leave Alpine territory so they could protect their lands closer to Rome.

THE LEGACY OF LANGUAGES

With the Romans gone, a flood of Germans washed into Switzerland. At the same time, another ethnic group, called Burgundians, invaded from the west. The two fought many battles on Swiss soil as they jockeyed for territory. Eventually, the French dialect spoken by the primarily Christian Burgundians replaced the Romans' Latin language in the portion of Switzerland they controlled. In their districts, the pagan Alemanni continued to converse in German.

That language legacy remains today. The western Swiss still speak French, and the northern and eastern Swiss speak German. In the far south of Switzerland, an area ignored by the invaders, many people retained Romansh. In the canton of Ticino, the language evolved from Latin to what is now Italian. Thus, four principal languages are spoken by the Swiss. French and German are the most prevalent. Most modern Swiss can speak at least two of the languages.

INVADERS AND REBELLION

In the ninth century A.D., all Switzerland came under the control of the Frankish Emperor Charlemagne ("Charles the Great") and his Holy Roman Empire. Charlemagne died in 814, and his territory in Switzerland was divided between two of his grandsons. Eventually, for lack of strong leadership, the empire declined, and Switzerland again was a battleground for numerous petty princes. Anyone strong enough grabbed what he could. Powerful noble families such as the Zahringen and Kyburg retained huge estates and maintained private armies.

Out of this confusion, the houses of Savoie and Hapsburg became dominant. After much political maneuvering to fill the power vacuum left after the decline of the Holy Roman Empire, Count Rudolf of Hapsburg was elected German emperor in 1273. He controlled most of Switzerland by the time of his death in 1291. To oversee his territory, Rudolf established a system of strict governors, many from Hapsburg lands in Austria.

Much of central Europe was under control of the Hapsburgs.

Two representations of William Tell; an illustration showing Tell and his son passing the governor's hat (left) and a statue that stands in Altdorf

However, economic conditions were grim in Switzerland. Crops had failed and trade was falling off. Objecting to high taxes during such trying times, the citizens in the remote valleys of Uri, Schwyz, and Unterwalden decided they had had enough.

On August 1, 1291, they sent emissaries to a secret meeting in a meadow at Rütli, overlooking the lake at Luzern. There they drew up an "Eternal Pact" of mutual allegiance and help. The conspirators wrote their document in Latin and fixed their seals to the paper. The old parchment, with its ringing call to freedom, was the first declaration of Swiss independence. It is exhibited in the archives of the canton of Schwyz. Today, August 1 is Swiss National Day.

The Hapsburgs were furious with the rebellion. Soldiers were sent into the mountains to teach the rebels a lesson. The legend of William Tell, a native of Uri, grew out of the turmoil. According to the story, Gessler, an Austrian governor who worked for the Hapsburgs, was very cruel. He supposedly ordered the Swiss to remove their hats whenever they passed his hat, which had been nailed to a post in the center of Altdorf, the canton's largest town. Tell refused to comply and as a punishment was ordered to shoot an apple off his son's head using a bow and arrow. Since Tell was an expert marksman, he easily accomplished the difficult shot. The angry Gessler imprisoned Tell, who later escaped and killed the governor in an ambush. This launched a bloody Swiss uprising against the Hapsburgs that went on for a century.

There is no proof that a real William Tell lived. But a play written about the legend by Friedrich Von Schiller, a German, in 1804 is very famous. An opera portraying the folk hero was composed in 1829 by the Italian Gioacchino Rossini.

THE CONFEDERATION OF THE EIGHT CANTONS

While there might not have been a Tell, there were many other Swiss heroes who held the Hapsburgs at bay in many battles. In 1315, Duke Leopold of Hapsburg decided to crush the rebellion. He sent a huge force of picked troops over the slopes of Morgarten, intending to destroy the town of Schwyz. Waiting for his well-equipped army of twenty thousand men were fourteen hundred irate peasants from the three rebelling cantons. They were armed with thick clubs, spears, and sharpened farm implements. The Swiss ambushed the enemy marching on the shores of a small lake, killing hundreds of them by rolling huge boulders and massive trees from the mountains above onto the trapped columns. The victory of Morgarten secured the legitimacy of their revolt.

Other cantons soon entered the confederation and took up the sword. Luzern joined in 1332, Zürich in 1351, Glarus and Zug in 1352, and Bern in 1353. The union was called the Confederation of the Eight Cantons.

The confederation continued to be harassed by the Hapsburgs. The fourteenth and fifteenth centuries were almost uninterrupted years of wars. The battles of Sempach in 1386 and Näfels in 1388 resulted in more defeats for the Hapsburgs.

With these victories, the Swiss gained an international reputation as fierce fighters who refused to compromise their values when it came to questions of independence.

However, the confederation remained economically poor, resulting in an enormous pool of unemployed young men. Many subsequently enlisted in the confederation army, making distinguished careers for themselves.

With this regular manpower reserve, the cantons reached out to secure more territory, hoping to defend both the Alpine passes and the plateau. From 1474 to 1477, the Swiss allied themselves with France and Austria against Burgundy, at this time an independent kingdom in what is now eastern France. The hard-fighting Swiss and their allies swept the field, crushed the Burgundian duke, Charles the Bold, and gained the territory that today makes up the canton of Vaud.

These bloody Burgundian wars were the first in which the Swiss actually hired themselves out to foreign governments as mercenaries, a practice that was to continue for several generations.

During this time, other territories applied for admission to the confederation. The first eight cantons always wrangled over the qualifications of each applicant, almost going to war several times. Nicholas of Flue, a quiet Swiss farmer who had a strong love for his people, appeared on the scene. Through his calm reasoning, Nicholas persuaded the Swiss leaders to resolve their differences by compromise rather than warfare.

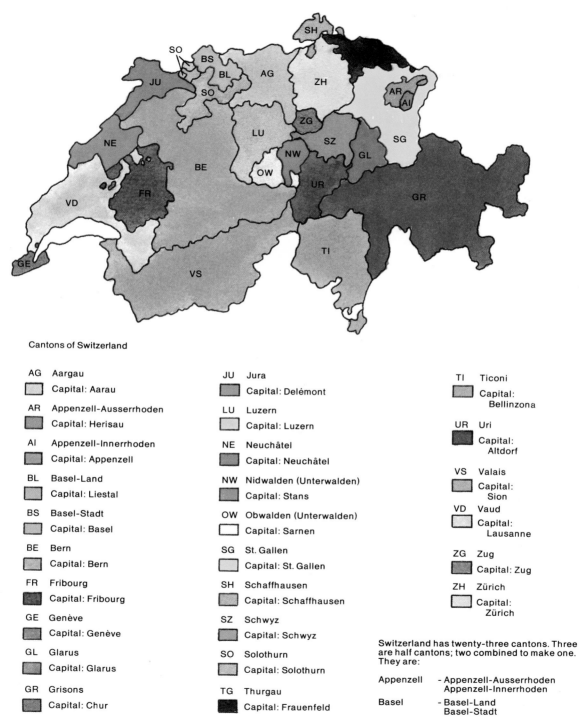

Cantons of Switzerland

AG Aargau	**JU** Jura	**TI** Ticoni
Capital: Aarau	Capital: Delémont	Capital: Bellinzona
AR Appenzell-Ausserrhoden	**LU** Luzern	**UR** Uri
Capital: Herisau	Capital: Luzern	Capital: Altdorf
AI Appenzell-Innerrhoden	**NE** Neuchâtel	**VS** Valais
Capital: Appenzell	Capital: Neuchâtel	Capital: Sion
BL Basel-Land	**NW** Nidwalden (Unterwalden)	**VD** Vaud
Capital: Liestal	Capital: Stans	Capital: Lausanne
BS Basel-Stadt	**OW** Obwalden (Unterwalden)	**ZG** Zug
Capital: Basel	Capital: Sarnen	Capital: Zug
BE Bern	**SG** St. Gallen	**ZH** Zürich
Capital: Bern	Capital: St. Gallen	Capital: Zürich
FR Fribourg	**SH** Schaffhausen	
Capital: Fribourg	Capital: Schaffhausen	
GE Genève	**SZ** Schwyz	
Capital: Genève	Capital: Schwyz	
GL Glarus	**SO** Solothurn	
Capital: Glarus	Capital: Solothurn	
GR Grisons	**TG** Thurgau	
Capital: Chur	Capital: Frauenfeld	

Switzerland has twenty-three cantons. Three are half cantons; two combined to make one. They are:

Appenzell – Appenzell-Ausserrhoden
Appenzell-Innerrhoden

Basel – Basel-Land
Basel-Stadt

Unterwalden – Nidwalden
Obwalden

A celebration of Swiss National Day, August 1, in Bürkli-Platz in Zürich. The whole country celebrates that national holiday with formal ceremonies and wonderful firework displays.

Under his guidance, the city-states of Fribourg and Solothurn were admitted to the confederation in 1481. Basel and Schaffhausen joined in 1501, followed by Appenzell in 1513. Later, Nicholas was honored by the grateful Swiss. He was canonized by the Catholic church in 1947 and made a patron saint of the country. His remains are in a church in Sachselm.

A NAME AND A FLAG

In the fifteenth century, the entire confederation was being called Schweizer, the name derived from the powerful canton of Schwyz. The words *Schweizer* or *Schwytz* are believed to stem from ancient terms meaning a "place of burning," or a "clearing by the fire for cultivation." They apparently refer to a method of removing forests before crops could be planted on the rocky Swiss soil. The words *Swiss* and *Switzerland* evolved from *Schweizer* and *Schweizer*-land.

The modern Swiss flag was also borrowed from Schwyz. Its white cross on a red square goes back to before the days of the confederation, when Schwyz was still under the thumb of outsiders. For their help in a war, Hapsburg King Rudolf I permitted the Schweizers to use the cross on their blood-red war banner. However, today's white cross stands for the Christianity of the Swiss nation.

At the battle of Laupen in 1339, the troops of Uri, Schwyz, and Unterwalden fought under this banner. From then on, the flag was semiofficial.

MERCENARIES: TAMERS OF KINGS

Throughout the sixteenth century, the Swiss flag was carried across many battlefronts. The demand for Swiss mercenary soldiers had increased to a point where fighting men had become the largest national export. They were called "tamers of kings" and would fight for anyone who would pay them well for their services. They marched under their own officers, regardless of where they were sent or in whose army they fought.

Eventually, however, this practice took a tragic turn. During a series of wars in Italy between 1500 and 1516, Swiss soldiers fought on both sides, and thousands were killed by their own compatriots. At the Battle of Marignano, waged near Milan in Italy on September 13 and 14, 1515, superior French forces devastated the confederation. This defeat convinced the Swiss that strict neutrality in international conflicts was the best protection for themselves as a small nation.

Swiss soldiers, either as individuals or as entire regiments, have fought in almost every war that has been waged in the past five hundred years, including the American Civil War.

For instance, the French King Francis I used 120,000 Swiss in his wars against Spain in the mid-1500s. His elite bodyguard was called the Hundred Swiss. Seven hundred Swiss soldiers and

The Lion of Luzern was designed by a Danish sculptor, Bertel Thorvaldsen.

twenty-six officers were massacred in 1792 during the French Revolution. They died while defending the Tuileries Palace in Paris from an attacking mob. Their heroism is remembered with a massive stone monument called the Lion of Luzern. The huge figure of a dying lion was carved out of a wall of rock near the Glacier Garden in Luzern.

The Swiss constitution of 1874 finally ended the practice of remuneration of Swiss by foreigners. Yet volunteering in foreign armies was not prohibited until 1927.

THE SWISS GUARD

The only exception to that ruling today is the colorful Swiss Guard, founded in 1505 by Pope Julius II. The 110-man unit is recruited from the Catholic cantons of Switzerland as bodyguards of the pontiff, who lives in Vatican City.

Swiss neutrality has proved to be as important a protection as the country's lofty mountain borders in all the decades since the 1500s. Switzerland has maintained this delicate policy even during both the terrible world wars that devastated Europe in the twentieth century.

Chapter 4

FROM WAR TO PEACE

The late Middle Ages in Europe were savage, turbulent times. There was barely any respite from war. Although geographically isolated, the Swiss were not able to escape the upheaval around them. In fact, the mercenaries of the cantons seemed to welcome the promise of adventure offered in the military, discounting the pain and suffering that often resulted. Besides being sought after for service in other armies, they were able to defeat every enemy attacking their fortress confederation.

At home, there were political quarrels and squabbles over the cantons' boundaries and access to commercial outlets. These disputes were settled more often by blood than by negotiations. Forgotten were the gentle admonitions of Nicholas of Flue, whose wise reasoning had settled many confrontations in the past.

THE REFORMATION: VOICES OF CHANGE

In the sixteenth century, a broadly based religious renewal movement swept Europe. This crusade, called the Reformation, shook the existing Christian world to its theological foundation. Demands for change in church structure and practices often took a violent turn. As a crossroads of ideas as well as geography,

Swiss Protestant reformer Ulrich Zwingli had supporters in Zürich, Glarus, and Schaffhausen.

Switzerland was involved in the controversy. The Reformation split the Swiss Confederation into Catholic and anti-Catholic factions.

It became a bitter period for Switzerland. Christianity had come to the cantons during Roman rule but had a difficult time when the land was overrun by pagan Germans. In the sixth and seventh centuries, Irish Catholic missionaries such as Saint Gallus returned to the ravaged countryside. Saint Gallus settled on the banks of the Stenach River and founded a magnificent Benedictine abbey there, around which blossomed the beautiful city of St. Gallen. Over the ensuing years, as Christianity reestablished itself, Swiss spirituality deepened.

Yet this depth of soul was not enough to prevent the era's terrible religious wars from claiming Switzerland as a victim. In addition to homegrown reformers, the country became a haven for refugees persecuted in their homelands because of religious beliefs.

Ulrich Zwingli was a Zürich priest who began loudly complaining about some Roman Catholic practices. Zwingli particularly objected to simony, the sale of papal indulgences. An indulgence granted by the Catholic pope is believed to lessen afterlife punishments for sins committed on earth. Unfortunately, some bishops and priests had grown rich by making their congregations pay for indulgences.

Zwingli broke away from Roman Catholicism and formed his own branch of Protestantism. A number of unhappy Catholics agreed with Zwingli and soon converted to his strict brand of religion. Most of his more ardent supporters came from Zürich, Glarus, and Schaffhausen.

Elsewhere in Switzerland, other reformers attacked the established church. In Bern, many churchgoers followed Berthold Haller. The people of Basel listened to John Hausschein. In Genève, French reformer Guillaume Farel attracted a large following. Each reformer had his own brand of spirituality, usually one at odds with the others as well as that of traditional Roman Catholicism.

JOHN CALVIN AND THE ELECT

The next voice added to the religious uproar was that of John Calvin. Calvin was a French Protestant who fled to Switzerland. His radical teachings were rejected at the University of Paris, where he had been a professor. One of Calvin's basic tenets claimed that the Bible was the only source of knowledge and authority in questions of religion. Calvin also said that people had no will of their own, that faith was the only thing that would save them from hell. Another of his more controversial theories stated that certain lucky persons, "the elect," were "predestined" to be sent to heaven after they died. This meant that only some individuals would be saved; everyone else was damned.

Another religious reformer was French-born Jean Calvin who operated out of the city of Genève.

Calvin established himself in Genève, and his hardworking, dedicated followers soon controlled the city. Calvin's Genève became Protestantism's Vatican City, the seat of Reformation power and influence. From Genève, missionaries and their new ideas flowed to England, Scotland, Bohemia, Hungary, and Holland.

RELIGIOUS WARS AND NEUTRALITY

However, the cantons of Solothurn, Fribourg, Uri, Schwyz, Unterwalden, Luzern, and Zug remained true to the established Catholic faith. Bloody battles erupted between adherents of the different religious philosophies. The wars dragged on for years. As a result, the nation of Switzerland remains evenly divided between Protestant and Catholic theologies. However, the hatreds of the past were put aside long ago. Today, the Swiss are very tolerant of each other's beliefs.

Despite those early religious disagreements, the Swiss remained neutral in other controversies ravaging Europe, due to a complex set of alliances with outside nations. In 1648, Switzerland's policy of neutrality was officially recognized in the Treaty of Westphalia, a pact that ended the Thirty Years War. That terrible conflict involved most of Europe in causes ranging from religious disputes to thirst for territorial expansion. Throughout it all, the Swiss minded their own business. At the end of the bloodshed, many of the warring nations were in shambles.

LONGINGS FOR INDEPENDENCE

Despite the guarantees of the Treaty of Westphalia, Switzerland did not enjoy internal peace. Some of the cantons grew wealthy and aggressively took advantage of their poorer, more rural neighbors. Several familes in Bern, Zürich, Luzern, and Basel gobbled up the political and economic power. They levied heavy taxes, which made life harsh for the workers and farmers. However, the peasants continually objected to the pressures and rebelled several times during the eighteenth century. But the rich families and powerful cantons had private armies that cruelly enforced the law and put down the peasants.

At that time clouds were gathering that would affect the political and economic fate of Europe. By 1781, American colonists had been successful in throwing off English rule. Then the French Revolution erupted in 1789. Word of far-reaching reforms initiated by those two rebellions quickly spread to other countries. The Swiss lower class subsequently copied their liberated neighbors in a furious uprising against their own aristocratic rulers.

In January 1798, the people of Vaud attacked an occupation army from Bern and proclaimed a new republic.

THE HELVETIAN REPUBLIC

Although the revolutionary armies of France supported reforms in their own country, their leaders sought territory that would be a protective buffer on their eastern flank. Besides, the wealthy cantons of Switzerland, except for French-speaking Roman Catholic Jura, were considered fair game, ripe for the plucking. In addition, some of the French-speaking Swiss wanted to be under French protection.

For these reasons, the French considered the Swiss upheaval as an excuse to invade the smaller confederation in March 1798. Not since the Roman occupation had such a major power attacked Switzerland and penetrated so deep into its territory.

Vaud's liberation therefore did not last long. It was one of the first cantons to be submerged by the mighty French army. The rest of Switzerland was soon overrun, and the confederation collapsed in a heap of faded dreams. In its place, the French established the Helvetian Republic, propped up by bayonets and muskets. Genève and other Swiss cantons were annexed by France.

NAPOLEONIC REGIME

Despite the heavy fist of the French occupiers, the Helvetian Republic did not function very well. The Swiss continually complained about the new system and did not cooperate with the invaders. Finally, in 1803, Napoleon Bonaparte intervened.

Napoleon was then in control of France, eagerly grasping for more European conquests. Whatever he said became law in French-occupied countries, a fact not appreciated by the independent-minded Swiss. By the Act of Mediation, he abolished the Helvetian Republic and established what he called a "federal regime." Six more cantons were added in 1803: St. Gallen, Grisons, Aargau, Thurgau, Ticino, and Vaud. Legislative power was given to a diet, or parliament, presided over by a chief *landammann*. This officer remained in his job for ten years. This centralization of power did not sit well with the Swiss, who were more comfortable with their traditional system of cantons.

Napoleon's power began slipping by 1812. Taking advantage of this, his enemy Austria sent an army into Switzerland and occupied Basel and Schaffhausen. The diet decided it would be best not to have anything to do with Napoleon. It annulled the federal regime. Some of the cantons wanted to go back to the old way of running things, with the rich families in power again.

However, the more independent cantons found a champion for their cause: Tsar Alexander I of Russia. At the Congress of Vienna in 1815, which ended Europe's wars with Napoleon, the tsar encouraged the Swiss to draw up a new confederation plan.

THE CONSTITUTION OF 1848

The proposal was adopted and the country's policy of neutrality reconfirmed. Three more cantons were added to the list in 1815: Valais, Neuchâtel, and Genève. Thus, after five hundred years, Switzerland finally stabilized its boundaries.

However, the cantons were stronger than the central government. Nobody wanted to listen to the diet. To add to the problems of government, religious difficulties arose again in the 1840s. Seven Catholic cantons broke away and formed the *Sonderbund*, a defensive alliance against the other Swiss cantons.

A short civil war resulted. But the central government, with

The original headquarters of the International Red Cross and its founder, Henri Dunant

troops led by a popular hero, General Guillaume-Henri Dufour, was victorious. In less than a month, the war was over with the loss of about 150 soldiers. The most important result of the Sonderbund War was the writing of a new federal constitution in 1848. That constitution, with revisions in 1874 and only minor changes since then, is still in force today.

HEADQUARTERS TO THE WORLD

After 1848, the Swiss turned their energies toward building a modern state. They have been able to remain neutral ever since, even during World Wars I and II. Because of the strict Swiss policy of not taking sides, many international organizations have established headquarters in the country. They range from the United Nation's World Health Organization in Genève to Zürich's Fédération Internationale de Football, the governing body of soccer-playing countries.

The International Red Cross, founded by Henri Dunant in 1863, has its headquarters in Genève. Its flag was adapted by the international community in 1864. A convention of European nations decided to invert the Swiss colors, making a red cross on a white background, for an easily recognizable sign of charity and protection for the wounded and prisoners of war.

Dunant also was instrumental in establishing rules of warfare called the Geneva Convention. The first Geneva Convention was signed by sixteen European countries in 1864. Other conventions, in 1906, 1929, and 1949, have refined the original treaty. It has been signed by most nations of the world.

Switzerland's cities host high-level conferences on many subjects, from nuclear disarmament to world hunger. Many important decisions affecting other nations are made in Switzerland. Everywhere are diplomats, researchers, and governmental bureaucrats from almost every country in the world. Representatives of oil-producing nations might be discussing how much to charge for their mineral wealth. Next door, the International Red Cross could be working on a plan to aid refugees.

SWISS INFLUENCE IN THE WORLD

The Swiss participate in many activities of the United Nations, although their country is not a member. They belong to such groups as the International Labor Organization, the World Meteorological Organization, and many internationally known charitable associations. The country often donates financial and technological help to nations in distress due to war or natural disaster.

Switzerland also represents the interests of others when diplomatic relations have been broken off between governments.

For instance, Switzerland represents at least ten nations that do not have embassies in Cuba. With their neutral image, the Swiss are great referees and often are asked to mediate disputes.

Yet the Swiss also look out for their own interests as well, especially in commercial ventures. In 1959, Switzerland joined the European Free Trade Association. In 1972, it signed other trade agreements with the European Community.

A DIVERSITY OF UNITED CANTONS

Politically, Switzerland is very different from most other countries. Each canton has its own traditions, its own outlook on life, and its own way of doing things.

Today's Switzerland is considered a league of democracies, meaning a collection of individual cantons—each with its own constitution and governing assembly. The addition of Jura in 1979 brought the number of cantons to twenty-three.

Three of the twenty-three cantons are divided into half-cantons, two combined to make one. They are Appenzell, a combination of Appenzell-Ausserrhoden and Appenzell-Innerrhoden; Basel, a combination of Basel-Land and Basel-Stadt; and Unterwalden, a combination of Nidwalden and Obwalden. The other cantons are Aargau, Bern, Fribourg, Genève, Glarus, the Grisons, Jura, Luzern, Neuchâtel, St. Gallen, Schaffhausen, Schwyz, Solothurn, Thurgau, Ticino, Uri, Valais, Vaud, Zug, and Zürich.

Over all is the federal government, headquartered in Bern. However, in Switzerland authority moves upward, not downward. The Federal Assembly, the Swiss parliament, receives all its authority from the voters. The Swiss can directly affect the administration of their country.

All changes in the constitution have to be submitted to the electorate for approval or rejection. A majority of national votes either way decides the outcome. A majority of voters in each canton also determines the response of the canton in parliament. All federal legislation, except emergency regulation, is technically subject to approval by the voters.

Most Swiss men and women appreciate this responsibility and jealously guard it. In Appenzell, Glarus, and Unterwalden, voting takes place in large assemblies in the open air called *landsgemeinde.*

FEDERAL GOVERNMENT

At the top is the federal government, with the Federal Assembly consisting of two chambers: the National Council, made up of two hundred representatives of the people; and the Council of States, with forty-six delegates from the cantons.

The highest executive body is the Federal Council, which consists of seven members elected by the legislature. Each member serves for four years and is responsible for a specific governmental department. Balance is preserved between representatives from Catholic and Protestant cantons and cantons that speak German, French, Italian, or Romansh.

The Federal Council elects the president of the Swiss Confederation. The president can serve only a one-year term.

The federal tribunal oversees the legal system. Elected by the Federal Assembly for six-year terms, the twenty-six members of the court sit in French-speaking Lausanne, rather than in Bern. This is another indication that the Swiss don't want to concentrate too much central authority in one area.

Thus, over the years, the Swiss have preserved their national unity and rugged individualism — from religion to politics.

Vacationers in Switzerland can enjoy leisurely living in
St. Moritz (above) or the thrill of hang gliding (below).

Chapter 5

OVER HILL
AND DALE

For the visitor, Switzerland holds delightful surprises. In one exciting day's trip, a visitor can experience mountainous polar conditions on the Jungfraujoch and a tropical atmosphere in lowland Lugano.

ST. MORITZ

Dozens of elegant resorts snuggle into the deep folds of the mountains or perch on the high slopes. Some of the more exotic vacation hideaways are in Brig, Arosa, Lenzerheide, and St. Moritz.

International celebrities enjoy visiting St. Moritz, which has been a tourist attraction for one hundred years. The Swiss say that the steamy mineral springs there were known three thousand years ago. In the Middle Ages, pilgrims would come from around Europe to escape summer heat and pestilence. But in the past century, fancy lodges and grand hotels have sprung up to attract a richer clientele.

Today's guests—film stars, royalty, business magnates—fancy the town's fine hotel service and the great sporting opportunities nearby, especially skiing. For visitors who want a real challenge, there is two-person hang gliding over the mountains, exciting and dangerous any time of the year, but especially in February's raw winds.

Winter horse races on the frozen lake near the St. Moritz train station are explosions of ice and hooves. The thoroughbreds pound around the turns on the lake. There is even a special event in which horses pull jockeys who wear tiny skis.

THE GRISONS

The Grisons (*Graubünden* in German) are in southeastern Switzerland, where the Rhine River is born. At least 150 valleys in the mountains make the landscape look like the blade of a jagged saw. This 2,800-square-mile (7,252-square-kilometer) canton is one of the most rugged in all Switzerland and is a linguistic crossroads where the residents speak German, Italian, or Romansh. Usually, the people can speak several languages.

There are many towering glaciers in the Grisons. One of the largest is the great Grialetsch glacier near a mountain called Piz Vadret. The ponderous, rock-flecked wall of ice is an awesome reminder that the land was once covered by a vast sheet of ice.

A hike along the rugged trails through the Swiss National Park in the Grisons brings an occasional view of such fabled animals as the ibex, a wild mountain goat with huge curving horns.

The Swiss are very concerned about preserving the natural beauty of their environment. All plants and trees in the 70-square-mile (113-square-kilometer) recreation area are protected by federal law. Camping is not allowed. All the trails, even in the most remote part of the park, are kept as neat and trim as if they were brushed and combed daily.

The Lenzerheide-Valbella area in the Grisons (left) is a popular ski area. The library of the Benedictine Abbey in St. Gallen (right) contains over 100,000 volumes, including one-thousand-year-old illuminated manuscripts.

ST. GALLEN

Eastern Switzerland is as lovely as a tapestry woven by the mills in St. Gallen. The canton's textile industry is known throughout the world for its quality and delicacy. The merchants and designers of the city of St. Gallen offer racks of gay silks, cottons, and linens, ready for clothing designers to craft into fashionable suits and dresses.

The capital city of St. Gallen canton is also called St. Gallen. A famous abbey of the Irish missionary Gallus was destroyed during the Reformation. But many of its ancient library books were rescued, and the structure was rebuilt to house the volumes, some of which are one thousand years old. St. Gallen's nearby baroque-style cathedral is heavy with gilt and marble. Statues of angels and saints peer down from every cornice.

51

The fertile countryside of Appenzell

APPENZELL

The countryside of the two half-cantons that make up Appenzell contains well-tended orchards, meadows, and fields. There are dairy cows there, many of them Brown Swiss, a breed prized for its milk. Neat farms are everywhere, with nothing out of place. Even the woodpiles look as if the logs had been cut and stacked by engineers. In the Toggenburg Valley is the town of Wildhaus, where religious reformer Ulrich Zwingli was born. His home is open for tours.

LAKE CONSTANCE

Not far from Appenzell is Lake Constance, sometimes called the Bodensee. This is one of the largest lakes in Europe, encompassing 208 square miles (539 square kilometers).

Sleek excursion boats ply the lake's unruffled greenish waters.

Brown Swiss cows (left) are prized for their milk.
Right: The medieval city of Schaffhausen

Vacationers relax in the bright sunlight as their vessels lazily drift past the Alpine panorama. The mountains in the distance are often shrouded in mist, obscuring their peaks. But on crisp, clear days, the mountains are visible, and almost every rock seems to stand out in the lake.

SCHAFFHAUSEN

Schaffhausen, capital of the northernmost canton of Switzerland, is a well-preserved medieval city on the banks of the Rhine River. The primarily Protestant canton is like a thumb of Switzerland poking into neighboring West Germany. The city is crowded with towers, parapets, castles, halls, and homes. Schaffhausen has long been a trading center and was once ruled by powerful medieval workers' unions and traders' guilds.

A statue honoring the women of Zürich (left) stands high above the city (right).

ZÜRICH

Zürich is the sprawling, mighty capital city of the canton of Zürich. It is the throbbing industrial heart of Switzerland and its largest urban area. There is no air pollution, however; all factories are run by electricity.

Zürich is a Protestant town, where Zwingli established his church. There is a large statue of the reformer alongside the Limmat River. The dour face of Zwingli is enough to frighten everyone into being on good behavior.

Yet streets in the nearby university quarter are packed with crowded bars and trendy rock clubs. Zürich's young people wear the latest fashions and tune their radios to whatever upbeat modern music is popular.

High atop the Lindenhof hill in the city center, a statue honors

Traffic along the Limmat River (left) and a flea market (right) in Zürich

the women of Zürich who saved the city from an attack by the
Austrians during the Middle Ages. The men of the town had been
driven away by the invaders, but the Zürich housewives refused
to surrender. They put on all the armor they could find and
marched to the top of the Lindenhof. From that lofty bastion, they
waved swords and spears, scaring the Austrians into thinking
another Swiss army was attacking. The statue on the hill
commemorates the bravery of those tough and fearless women.
Today the hill is much more peaceful, a retreat from the rush of
traffic and clamor of city noise. Nursemaids and baby-sitters often
bring children to the hill to play.

In 1953, an exciting program for children started in Zürich: the
Kinder Cirkus Ullalla-Bassissi, a children's circus. Every summer
more than three hundred young people tour the country,
performing acrobatics, tumbling, juggling, and animal acts. The

money that is collected goes to the Pestalozzi Children's Village, a home for orphans in Trogen near St. Gallen.

The home is named for Johann Heinrich Pestalozzi, a Zürich-born educational reformer. A statue of him sits quietly in a tiny park on the Bahnhofstrasse, the city's bustling main street. The monument depicts him with a little boy at his side. Pestalozzi believed that every youngster has unique gifts that should be encouraged and developed in school. He was also a firm advocate of such subjects as natural sciences, even for very young pupils. His theories have been accepted by educators around the world.

Zürich is the hub of the Swiss transportation system. Its airport is more than just a landing place for planes. It also has a four-level underground train station, providing the latest in transportation connections. More than 180 trains pass through the airport every day. Tourists can book their bags at one hundred stations along Swiss rail routes. Baggage is transferred to the travelers' airplanes, where it can be picked up upon arriving at the plane's destination.

LUZERN

Luzern, sometimes called "Queen of Swiss Resorts," lies in central Switzerland and is the capital city of the canton of Luzern. The eight-hundred-year-old city earned its regal title for centuries of royal catering to travelers. Even now, ornate hotels and casinos attract international visitors.

Luzern is a water city. Paddleboats and rowboats can be rented along the Schweizerhofquai on the north side of the lake. The little craft then scoot about, keeping well out of the way of the larger tour boats that can travel far out on the blue-green lake. Two covered bridges cross the River Reuss, which connects with

In Luzern, the Mill Bridge (left)
and a square in the old section (right)

the lake. One is the Chapel Bridge, built in 1367. Its gables are brightly decorated with hand-painted scenes from Swiss history. The other is the Mill Bridge, built in 1408, with a dramatic painting called "Dance of Death."

On the north side of the lake is the medieval old town with watchtowers, a high city wall, and narrow streets. Wandering in the early evening through the Kornmarkt, the central square, it is not surprising to hear the lonely wail of a saxophone. The cry of a modern jazz tune somehow does not seem out of place in this ancient city, noted for its music festivals. The "new town" is on the south shore, with the railroad station, lake steamer docks, and a theater.

The Lion of Luzern monument is a huge statue of a dying lion, carved out of a cliff. It honors the Swiss Guards of Louis XVI who were massacred in the French Revolution. The monument is close

*Visitors in Luzern can stroll in the city or
take a cogwheel train to nearby Mount Pilatus.*

to the Glacier Garden, a series of large potholes dug into the rock
by the ancient ice sheet. An Ice Age Museum, with much
information about glaciers, is adjacent to the gardens.

Luzern has Europe's largest transport museum, with displays
from horse-drawn carts to a lunar exploration vehicle. Inside it is
another museum that displays the paintings and graphic art of
Hans Erni, a Luzern artist from the twentieth century.

The neighborhood around the Lake of Lucerne is William Tell
country. The German term for the lake is *Vierwaldstättersee*, "Lake
of the Four Cantons." It is surrounded by the cantons of Uri,
Schwyz, Unterwalden, and Luzern. An impressive statue of the
legendary Swiss hero Tell stands in the village of Altdorf.

The highest mountain in the area is Mount Pilatus, at 6,995 feet
(2,131 meters). According to legend, buried near the peak is
Pontius Pilate, the Roman governor who had Jesus Christ put to

Tourist boats ply Lake Lucerne.

death. At the west end of Lake Lucerne is an electric cogwheel train that chunks and rumbles its jerky way to the top of the mountain. The trip takes about a half hour from the village of Alpnachstad. High in the mountain reaches is a panoramic view of the city of Luzern. Even in the summer, snow can be found hidden in shadowy glens and pockets between the rocks.

BASEL

Basel, the capital of the canton of Basel-Stadt, is on the banks of the Rhine River in northern Switzerland. This is Switzerland's port, connected by the Rhine to the major inland ports of Europe and on to the North Sea. It is the heart of Europe's intertwined railroad and highway network, tucked into a border area abutting Germany and France. Tourists like to walk around a marker post

The Rhine flows north through the city of Basel.

set into a field where the frontiers join, thereby crossing the territory of three nations in just a few seconds. The border is a mere 3 miles (4.8 kilometers) from the city center.

Six bridges span the Rhine, linking the city's neighborhoods. The Gros-Basel (Greater Basel) side has towering commercial and cultural buildings, while the opposite side is Klein-Basel (Little Basel), the industrial district with chemical plants and other factories. Along the Rheinweg, a leafy pathway beside the river, strollers can watch heavily laden, bulky barges on their 500-mile (805-kilometer) journey up the Rhine.

Basel has been known as a merchants' town since the Middle Ages. Because of its location, it has always been at the crossroads of trade. Its favored position also attracted many fresh ideas from the outside world. The city is honored to have the oldest university in Switzerland, founded by Pope Pius II in 1460. Artists and craft workers who live in the city now have made Basel a cultural showpiece for Switzerland, filling the numerous galleries with pottery, sculpture, paintings, and weavings.

The Gothic fountain in Fish Market Square (left) in Bern
Above: One of the buildings of the University of Basel

The *Drei Könige am Rhein* (Three Kings on the Rhine) Hotel is the oldest hotel in Switzerland, dating back to 1036. Such famous personages as Napoleon and Princess Victoria (who became Queen Victoria of England), have been guests there. Today's visitors can enjoy sitting on the hotel terrace, munching on a pastry made of honey, kirsch, almonds, and hazelnuts.

BERN

The seat of government in the Swiss Confederation is Bern, the city of bears. It is also the capital of the canton of Bern. In German, the name is pronounced almost like the plural word for bear, *baren*. The city's heraldic symbol is, of course, a bear. A legend relates how in 1191 the Duke of Zahringen sent an exploring party to find the site for a new city. According to the story, they were to name the town after the first animal they killed, which happened to be a bear.

The Bear Pit (left) and the Parliament Building (right) in Bern

On Sundays, youngsters take treats to the Bear Pit near the Nydegg Bridge, where bears have been exhibited since 1315. The ponderous creatures are smug performers who demand treats for their acrobatics.

Bern is the most flower conscious of Swiss cities. In the spring and summer, rainbows of roses and geraniums explode from window boxes, parks, and walkways.

The Clock Tower of Bern is a mechanical masterpiece, with moving figures to help tell the time. The little characters were added to the structure in 1530. A drummer, a piper, marching bears, and knights thump and whoomp from their lofty perch every hour. In the center, Father Time bangs out the rhythm with his scythe.

The Bernese Oberland hills roll around the city like the swell of sea waves. Thick stands of pine dapple the edges of the hills,

A view of Bern's famous Clock Tower (left) and a view from it (right) looking toward the Aare River

wherever the wheat fields end. The lakes are so dark blue as to be almost black. From a distance, tiny villages appear to have been painted on the landscape instead of being constructed of stone and wood. In fact, many artists have used the scenery as inspiration.

INTERLAKEN

Another town in the canton of Bern is Interlaken, well known for its summer music performances. The town straddles two lakes: Thunersee on the west and Brienzersee on the east. From the city's main street, residents can see the snow-frosted towers of the Jungfrau. The mountain is one of the most famous in Switzerland, rearing above its lowlier neighbors at 13,642 feet (4,138 meters). A mountain railway struggles upward to 11,333 feet (3,454 meters), making it one of the highest points in Europe reached by rail.

Clockwise from top left: A policeman in front
of a newsstand in Lausanne, carriage drivers in Interlaken,
skiing in the Alps, and the harbor at Neuchâtel

Near Interlaken is the towering peak called Schilthorn. A half-hour cable car rises to the pinnacle, some 9,750 feet (2,971 meters) above sea level. The cable car and the mountain backdrop were featured in a James Bond adventure movie.

JURA

The French-speaking canton of Jura is famous for downhill skiing, with its slopes a sweep of brightly colored schussers. On sharp winter afternoons, it looks as if a bag of confetti has been sprinkled across the glaring white snow. This region of western Switzerland is also well known for breeding fine horses, which grow pleasingly plump and strong on the lush Alpine grasses. Many manor houses and castles are sprinkled across the landscape, adding a delicately elegant touch to the scenery.

NEUCHÂTEL

Neuchâtel, the capital of Neuchâtel canton, fronts on a lake. Homes perched on hills overlook it, the largest lake wholly within Switzerland's borders. The craft of watchmaking began here in the eighteenth century and grew into a profitable industry. The Swiss Watchmaking Research Laboratory is here.

THE CANTON OF VAUD

Lausanne, the capital of Vaud, is on the north side of Lake Geneva (Lac Léman). It is known primarily for its cathedral, considered the finest Gothic building in Switzerland. Construction of the Cathedral of Notre Dame was begun in the twelfth century.

*The Gothic Cathedral
of Notre Dame
in Lausanne was
consecrated in 1275.*

It has five towers and a beautiful thirteenth-century, stained-glass rose window.

Another city in Vaud, Montreux, is a resort on Lake Geneva. The nearby snowcapped mountains protect the city, giving it a mild climate. In its gardens are magnolias and palm trees.

GENÈVE

Genève, the capital of the canton of the same name, is the third-largest city in Switzerland. Like Zürich, it became a Protestant town during the Reformation. In 1917, the city completed a monument to some of the great theologians from that era. The memorial is a row of stern-faced men carved from rock: Guillaume Farel, Jean Calvin, Théodore de Bèza, and John Knox. Farther along the wall are other Protestant figures, such as the English statesman Oliver Cromwell. The grim faces on the

The jet of water (above) in Lake Geneva rises over 400 feet (120 meters).
It is on daily from May to September. Below: The European headquarters
of the United Nations with the Woodrow Wilson Memorial in the foreground.

The central part of the Reformation Monument in Genève features statues of Théodore de Bèze, Jean Calvin, Guillaume Farel, and John Knox, great leaders of the Reformation.

monument look over a city that now can enjoy nightlife and even a bit of gambling in the casinos, quite unheard of in Calvin's day. Youngsters in the park find that the broad, hard stomachs of the statues make superb backboards for bouncing balls.

Genève, however, is known for more than its religious history. It has become the center of Swiss watchmaking.

In addition, Genève has a reputation as a host for diplomats. The Palais de Nations, where the League of Nations met after World War I, is now used as an office for its successor, the United Nations. Other international organizations, such as the YMCA, the Boy Scouts, the World Council of Churches, and the International Labor Office, are headquartered there as well.

TICINO

It's sometimes difficult to imagine Ticino as part of Switzerland. This canton, on the southern side of the Alps, is the only canton in which Italian is primarily spoken. Three famous resorts have made the district very popular with tourists: Lugano, Locarno, and Ascona. Even in the winter, the valleys are sheltered from

Houses crowd the shore of Lake Lugano (left). The Castle of Visconti Dukes of Milan in Locarno, now partially restored and used as a museum

harsh northern winds, which makes them popular with sun worshipers. Although the Italian touch might be puzzling at first, the canton's connection to Switzerland stretches back to the fourteenth century.

Medieval castles testify to the military link that once was necessary to protect the Swiss Confederation's southern borders. Various northern cantons battled over control of the rich Ticino lands, each building its own fortification. Three of the better known are the Uri, Schwyz, and Unterwalden castles.

All the bloodshed of those wild days is forgotten now, except by tour guides who go into great detail about princes and generals who once marched over the countryside. Today, visitors are more concerned with the September grape harvest and wine festivals. The town of Lugano greets its guests with floral decorations, costumed bands, yodeling, and almost bottomless carafes of red and white wines.

Switzerland is world famous for its banking industry. There are more than sixteen hundred banks throughout the country. Banks may be old or modern, like the one above in Zürich.

Chapter 6

LAND OF MILK
AND MONEY

The industriousness of the Swiss is their most valuable natural resource. They have learned to make do with what they have.

The Swiss specialize in research, planning, and assembling of goods. They have moved into highly technical fields that do not require the spread of huge factories and shelters. There is also a concentration of brainpower in banking, insurance, and other white-collar professions.

To live, the Swiss must export. To export, they have to rely both on goods they can produce and on services they can provide to the outside world. They concentrate on quality, a long-standing tradition.

BEGINNINGS OF INDUSTRIALIZATION

By the end of the nineteenth century, Switzerland was the most highly industrialized of all European countries. In the late 1870s, a majority of Swiss were urban workers instead of farmers. This phenomenon did not occur elsewhere on the European continent until at least fifty years later.

The process took generations of refinement. At first, there were problems. Although medieval Swiss merchants were considered the shrewdest in Europe, there was little manufacturing and much internal feuding between cantons. This meant that the early confederation was not economically strong. For instance, tolls or customs duties had to be paid when moving from canton to canton. It became cheaper to haul goods around Switzerland, rather than through the country.

It took the textile manufacturers and the watchmakers to place Switzerland on a more stable footing. Along with Swiss bankers, they struggled to make Switzerland competitive in the world market. Through necessity, the Swiss learned the hard lessons of cooperating and specializing in order to survive.

In the business world, Switzerland is noted for its emphasis on high technology and the production of precision machinery. The Swiss are thinkers and tinkerers who have invented the zipper, cellophane, rack railways, and rollers for grinding grain. Their merchandise ranges from massive diesel engines for marine propulsion to carnival and theme-park rides.

Swiss researchers and engineers have improved products. As an example, the Sulzer weaving machine replaced the old-fashioned bobbin with gripper projectiles to speed the production of cloth. The development of textile dyes led to the explosive growth of the pharmaceutical industry. If they believe in a product, Switzerland's shrewd investment bankers can marshal vast amounts of capital to underwrite new techniques and ideas.

Raw materials for industrial development, such as oil, iron ore, and coal, must be imported. To minimize their dependence on outside energy sources, the Swiss have built four nuclear power plants but still depend heavily on the nation's abundant water supply to run more than four hundred hydroelectric plants. The first hydroelectric generators were constructed in Baden, near

A ski boot factory in Wengen, a year-round resort area

Zürich. Today, the multinational firm of Brown Boveri is still headquartered there, producing 135,000-kilowatt turbo generators, the largest such machines in the world.

Swiss workers are versatile. Some manufacture electrical machinery, and scientific and optical instruments. Others make metal products—anything from pots to tractors. Still others work with chemicals and pharmaceuticals or in watchmaking.

WATCHMAKING: SMALL-SCALE SKILL

Watchmaking was introduced by French religious émigrés called Huguenots. These skilled, hardworking Protestants were named after their leaders, Bezanson Hugues, a Genève reformer. Calvinism prevented the French silversmiths and goldsmiths from making religious objects such as chalices, so they had to turn to

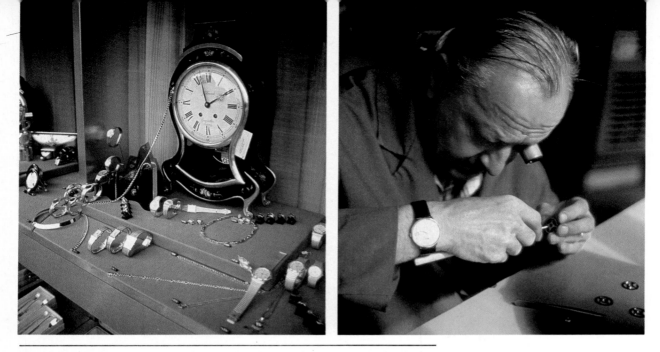

The technicians who work in the watchmaking industry are highly skilled.

some other craft and gradually took up watchmaking. In 1679, Daniel Jean Richard, made the first Swiss clock and went on to found his own company.

Watchmaking is a perfect industry for the Swiss, calling for skilled small-scale precision work. It doesn't take a lot of raw materials. The finished product is easy to transport.

The nation makes more than 105 million timepieces and movements each year. Of every ten watches made in the world, seven originate in Switzerland. They range from tiny pocket watches to "atomic clocks" measuring millionths of a second. Swiss scientists are always working on new timekeeping devices. The Swiss Laboratory for Horological Research in Neuchâtel was organized in 1962. Detailed work is undertaken here in miniaturization, lubrication, and metals.

Among the internationally recognized quality producers of watches are Longines, Omega, and Rolex. To counter low-priced competition from elsewhere, however, even the Swiss have had to

Sandoz chemical factory in Basel

make some refinements. More plastic instead of brass, for instance, is being used for some watch components. Cheap digital quartz watches, which became popular in the late 1970s, are also carving inroads into the traditional windup dial clock and watch markets. Yet even Swiss quartz watches are highly praised for their craftsmanship.

OTHER INDUSTRIES AND PRODUCTS

Other industries are more concentrated than is watchmaking. Three major firms are world-renowned pharmaceutical and chemical producers: Hoffman-La Roche, Sandoz, and Ciba-Geigy. They produce pesticides, insecticides, dyes, and similar products. Two other firms, Givaudan and Firmenich, manufacture substances used for perfumes.

Leopold Ruzicka, a science professor at Zürich's Federal Institute of Technology, was the first to synthetically produce musk, a basic element in making perfume. For his work with polymethylenes, he won the Nobel Prize in chemistry in 1939.

The textile and clothing industry is just as important. Weavers in Basel pioneered the use of fast looms in the sixteenth century. The looms helped give them an edge over the competition. There were so many textile companies by the 1700s that they were grudgingly nicknamed the "Swiss Nation" by their competitors.

Delicate Swiss embroidery also has been well known for centuries. Today, the industry is affected by tough competition from Third World countries. But the Swiss are confident that quality products will help them retain a major share of the high-fashion market, which accounts for about a third of Swiss exports.

Swiss corporations may seem small in comparison with those in other nations. But they are more extensive than they appear on the surface. A majority of stock in the companies is always held by Swiss citizens. Through foreign subsidiaries and licensing contracts, Swiss firms such as Nestlé are found all over the world. Nestlé makes chocolate goods, Nescafe products, and infant formula. Henri Nestlé, a chemist and pharmacologist, turned raw milk into a powder and developed one of the first baby foods. His corporation today is among the largest in Switzerland.

BANKING AND INSURANCE

There are also "invisible" industries in Switzerland. One of the foremost is financial. Dozens of bank facades line Zürich's Bahnhofstrasse, the city's main street. Heavy brass nameplates gleam outside the massive doors of these stolid institutions, emphasizing an impression of wealth and stability. There are more than sixteen hundred banks throughout the country, including the Swiss National Bank, commercial banks, state-owned banks in the cantons, and family-owned private banks.

Wealthy people from other countries often keep their money in

Swiss accounts. Because of Switzerland's neutrality, its banks are considered very safe. Depositors are assigned numbers for identification, thereby keeping their names secret. If a bank employee tells about any of these accounts, he or she can be imprisoned and fined.

Swiss insurance companies are also important pegs in the Swiss economy. The Swiss Reinsurance Company, founded in 1863, is one of the biggest in the world. It even paid claims to Americans after the San Francisco earthquake of 1906.

More than a hundred insurance firms are headquartered in Switzerland. They handle life, auto, marine, accident, transport, and other forms of coverage. About a quarter of the firms are foreign owned, but are supervised by Swiss federal authorities.

TOURISM: GOOD THINGS TO SEE

Ever since the first wandering tribes paused in Switzerland, tourists have been welcome. The Swiss knew they had the scenery, so they decided to promote it. More than forty million visitors swarm over the country annually, looking for skiing, health spas, sailing, hiking, or simply opportunities for relaxing.

Recently, there have not been enough workers in the service industries to accommodate this influx. A training hotel in Ascona was opened in 1973 to educate people interested in the lodging industry. An older hotel school is located at Chalet-à-Gobet, near Lausanne. With their intensive training, excellent Swiss hotel personnel have been welcome around the world.

Swiss accommodations range from the fabulous Kulm in St. Moritz to family-owned hideaways in the mountains. The Kulm, built in 1859, was the first building in Switzerland to use electric

The Jungfrau Railway takes skiers up to Kleine Scheidegg, near Bern, for spring skiing (left). The alpenhorn (above) is used by herders for calling their cattle.

lights. Showing extra finesse, the Dolder Hotel in Zürich daily flies in fresh tulips from Holland and roses from Israel for its dining room centerpieces.

Promoting all the good things about the country is the Swiss National Tourist Office, with headquarters in Zürich. The Swiss Tourism Federation studies the economic impact of this industry in Switzerland.

AGRICULTURE: CATTLE AND CHEESE

Despite the harsh landscape, agriculture still has a place in Switzerland. The land more often is suitable for pastureland than for farming. The country produces only about 55 percent of its own food; the rest has to be imported. Yet it has been dangerous for Switzerland to rely on outside sources for food. During the bleak days of World Wars I and II, neutral Switzerland often went hungry when supplies from abroad were curtailed. Consequently,

Cattle grazing in mountain meadows (left) and queen cows (right) parading to summer pasture in Lauterbrunnen Valley

Swiss farming initiative has turned inward. Today, large accessible farm plots are cultivated, rather than small out-of-the-way fields that are hard to harvest. Mechanization has taken over in all aspects of farming, increasing output on the arable land of the rolling Swiss plateau. This is the best agricultural land, stretching 150 miles (241 kilometers) by 30 miles (48 kilometers) near the Jura Mountains.

The grazing lands in the mountains are great for dairy cattle, which are highly regarded. In Appenzell, Schwyz, and other cantons, the animals are decked out with flowers and led by musicians to the summer pastures. The herders stay in the pastures with their animals all summer. Each animal in the herd wears a bell, to make it easy to find in case it wanders off.

Several breeds are popular, among them the Brown Swiss. This tan-colored cow is found primarily in eastern and central Switzerland. The white and tawny spotted cow, the Simmental, is found in western Switzerland. The brown-black Eringer is one of the oldest breeds in the world.

A display of cheese

In the past, cheese making was the best means of disposing of milk, and cheese became an item of barter. In the years of horse-drawn vehicles, the Swiss had to import much of the fodder for the dray animals that trudged along the highways. They traded cheese to international brokers of hay and oats. From this basic trade came the roots of today's extensive dairy industry.

There are more than one hundred varieties of cheese produced today in fifteen hundred small dairies. Each dairy is headed by a master cheese maker who must go to school and earn a federal degree. The cheese is made only from fresh, natural milk and is carefully cured to develop a specific flavor and texture.

Since Swiss-produced cheese is totally a natural product without additives or chemicals, its color and taste vary depending on the season, area, and type of feed used. Emmenthaler cheese has a sweetish, nutlike flavor and is delicious in fondue. Another fondue cheese is Gruyère, which has a buttery taste. Appenzeller, sharp and tangy, is treated with a spiced white wine during its maturing. Raclette is soft and mild. Sapsago is a pungent herb

80

Vineyards near Lake Geneva

cheese from the canton of Glarus, made with a special clover called *ziegerkleepulver*. Royalp, sbrinz, spalen, tête de moine, vacherin fribourgeois, vacherin Mont d'Or, tomme vaudoise, and others have even more tongue-twisting names.

The Swiss grow a great deal of apples, pears, cherries, and other fruit, especially in Neuchâtel. Potatoes and sugar beets are other important crops. Wine grapes are cultivated in the milder areas of Switzerland around the shores of Lake Geneva, along the Rhone River, and in Ticino. Wine has been produced in western and southern Switzerland since the first century B.C. At Vevey, a major wine market, a festival is held every twenty-five years to celebrate the lowly grape.

WOODLAND: PROTECTING TREES

About a quarter of Switzerland is forested. The trees save the valleys by breaking up and diverting avalanches, erosion, and rockfalls before much damage is done. Consequently, there is little

Automobile drivers pass through the St. Gotthard Tunnel as they cross the mountains at 6,935 feet (2,114 meters) above sea level.

lumbering in Switzerland. On the lowlands, the forests protect the fragile croplands from the raw breath of the *föhn*, the seasonal hot, dry breeze out of the mountains. Acid rain, the result of auto exhaust and other pollution, has been blamed for the destruction of some Swiss woodland. Swiss scientists are studying the problem, which affects many other Western nations.

ROADS AND RAILROADS

An extensive transportation network links all parts of Switzerland. But in the old days, many of the high passes were blocked by snow for the winter. In 1049, a community of monks founded a hospice to house travelers in the Grand Saint Bernard Pass, which is 8,101 feet (2,469 meters) high. For search-and-rescue missions, they bred huge Saint Bernard dogs that would slog through blizzards to locate lost persons.

Today, the country is connected to the outside world by tunnels cut through the mountains. It took ten years to complete the 10.5-mile (17-kilometer) St. Gotthard Tunnel to Ticino, at a cost of 686 million Swiss francs. At regular intervals, television cameras keep

The St. Gotthard Pass road has many hairpin turns.

an eye on the traffic. The Furka Tunnel on the Furka-Oberalp Railway is the only year-round east-west connection through the Alps. It was opened in 1982, connecting the valleys of Goms, Urseren, and Tavetsch.

In 1844, the first train chugged into Switzerland. Ever since, the country has had a love affair with railroads. Today, all trains are electrified, running over a total network of 3,107 miles (5,000 kilometers), most of which is operated by the Swiss Federal Railways. Of the total, 2,240 miles (3,605 kilometers) are regular gauge and 870 miles (1,400 kilometers) are narrow gauge. While it is not easy running a railroad over and around Switzerland's landscape, the services are unmatched. For example, on the up-and-down journey of the Alpine Glacier Express, special glasses

Swiss railway

are used in the dining car. Their stems are at an angle, which keeps liquid from spilling on inclines. But the tilted glasses look strange when the train travels over flatland.

Engineers must constantly be on the alert for rock slides, avalanches, and even a stray cow or two on the tracks.

Automobile travel is almost as easy as riding the trains. There are good roads and well-maintained, carefully patrolled tunnels. However, in winter storms, sometimes automobile travel is impossible.

MARITIME AND AIR ECONOMY

The Swiss even have a merchant marine. The country ranks fiftieth among more than a hundred nations that operate fleets. This might be a surprise, considering Switzerland doesn't have an ocean port, but some five hundred barges and tugs flying the Swiss flag haul goods to the North Sea via the Rhine River. The country has long been interested in ocean travel because it was

A Swissair DC-10

economically more feasible to ship goods by Swiss-owned vessels. In the mid-1980s, thirty-one tankers and freighters were in the country's merchant fleet.

A secondary branch of Switzerland's maritime economy includes firms that construct or operate port installations in other nations, insurance firms, and docking companies. One Swiss company is the world's leading installer of ship engines.

In 1931, the Swiss national airline, Swissair, was formed by the merger of two air transport companies. Swissair's modern carriers accommodate more than seven million passengers a year. Several charter companies also operate within Switzerland, flying mostly smaller aircraft.

Switzerland is a bustling, prosperous land because its people work hard. They eagerly look for new and better ways of doing things and are not shy about adapting ideas from the outside to their own uses. The Swiss are very inventive, a trait that contributes to the economic success of a rockbound nation.

Clockwise from above:
a driver of a horse-drawn taxi,
Italian tourists, a Swiss
child, a shopper at the
market, and children in
native costumes

Chapter 7

THE BUSY SWISS

Over six million people live in Switzerland. More than a million residents of Switzerland are foreigners, perhaps diplomats or employees of the many non-Swiss corporations with offices in the country. As with many other industrialized European nations, Switzerland has long suffered from a shortage of native workers. Therefore, for the past century migrant laborers have been encouraged to come to Switzerland.

FOREIGN WORKERS

In the late 1800s, when the first railroad tunnels were blasted through the hard core of the Alps, Italians did much of the labor, and Swiss engineers supervised the operations.

Even today, Switzerland's Italian neighbors consider the Alpine country a fine place to work. Many have gone into service as waiters and waitresses, hotel desk clerks, bellmen, and chefs in Swiss resorts and hotels. In addition to the Italians, thousands of Greeks, Yugoslavs, Spaniards, and Turks have flocked to Zürich, Genève, St. Gallen, and other Swiss cities. Many of these thrifty, hardworking people attain a standard of living in Switzerland higher than they could have achieved by remaining in their home country. They own cars and television sets and carefully save a healthy chunk of their wages to send to their families.

But all Swiss streets are not paved with gold. Since it is expensive to live in Switzerland, some foreign workers live in poorer housing than the Swiss themselves. Many are single men who reside in small, crowded apartments near their place of employment. It is also financially impossible to bring their wives and children, so the laborers can become very lonely. Besides, immigrant workers have to live in some cantons for a prescribed time before their families can join them. In addition to these hardships, they must cope with what they consider strange food and customs. Even the languages may be unfamiliar at first.

Most foreigners cannot vote because they are not citizens. Only in Neuchâtel and Aargau can non-Swiss vote in cantonal elections. However, throughout the country, the workers receive their fair share of old-age and survivors' insurance and pension funds, since they contribute to the financial stability of the plans. About 20 percent of the total social security input is made by foreigners working in Switzerland.

FOREIGN VISITORS

Switzerland has always been a melting pot and a crossroads of cultures and traditions. The country has long been a haven for refugees. From their secure hideaways, political plotters could plot, writers could write, and dreamers could dream. German composer Richard Wagner lived in Switzerland for a time. So did Italian revolutionaries Giuseppe Garibaldi and Giuseppe Mazzini, Russian anarchist Mikhail Bakunin, and Communist leader Vladimir Lenin. Early in the twentieth century, Benito Mussolini took up residence but was expelled because of his revolutionary activities.

Irish novelist James Joyce is buried in Zürich. Scientist and mathematician Albert Einstein, a German, worked in Bern for the Swiss Patent Office while he was developing his theory of relativity. A lengthy list of brilliant minds have used Switzerland as a jumping-off point for their philosophies, a refuge from persecution, or a debating site for ideas.

SWISS ÉMIGRÉS

On the other hand, just as foreign workers flock to Switzerland, Swiss emigrate to work elsewhere in the world. Swiss citizens abroad are nicknamed the "Fifth Switzerland." The first four, of course, refer to the four major language groups: German, French, Italian, and Romansh. The existence of the Fifth Switzerland was recognized in 1966 by a constitutional amendment.

In the mid-1980s, at least 354,232 Swiss citizens lived in 168 different countries. Émigrés are usually specialists of some kind who return home when their tour of duty is completed.

This Swiss wanderlust has a long tradition. As early as 1719, the Simonius Vischer Company, a Swiss firm, was sending its hardy representatives wherever an untapped market held the promise of a profit. These eager salesmen traded in wool, spices, leather, fabrics, and vegetable dyes throughout Europe and deep into Asia. In nineteenth-century Japan, the Swiss merchant Siber Hegner was the biggest exporter of pearls to the United States.

Other Swiss became tutors to kings, confectioners for a hungry world, and master builders. They designed marble palaces in glittering St. Petersburg of Imperial Russia and hacked out homesteads in dense Brazilian jungles. Henry Haller has been, since 1963, the head cook at the White House in Washington, D.C.

Some émigrés took up new nationalities in their adopted lands. The soaring spans of the Hell Gate, George Washington, and Verrazano-Narrows bridges in New York City were the work of Zürich-born engineer Othmar Hermann Ammann. He moved to the United States in 1904 and became a citizen in 1924. Ammann was also a consultant in the building of San Francisco's famed Golden Gate Bridge.

UNIONS OF WORKERS

Switzerland is a nation of employees. Fewer than 10 percent of the population are in business for themselves. About 10 percent of the total work force cultivate farms. The others are in industry, tourism and service jobs, and financial or similar professional occupations. About one third belong to a union.

Most of the important unions—such as the Federation of Metalworkers and Watchmakers—are under the umbrella of the Swiss Federation of Trade Unions, consisting of 450,000 members. A second group, with about 100,000 workers, is represented by the Swiss Confederation of Christian Trade Unions. White-collar or professional workers usually belong to a union in the Federation of Swiss Employees' Societies.

The employers also have their own organizations: the Central Federation of Swiss Employers' Associations, the Swiss Association for Commerce and Industry, and the Swiss Federation of Arts and Crafts.

The independent Swiss Peasants' Union represents almost all the agriculture sector, from stockbreeders to milk processors. The

A TV camerawoman at work

Union of Swiss Producers is a splinter group, mostly from the French-speaking portion of the country.

Over the years, the bosses and the workers have argued. But on the whole, they have a fairly good relationship. Industrial disputes are usually settled peacefully by collective bargaining and so there are very few strikes.

The watchmakers and their employers agreed in 1937 not to have strikes but to talk out their problems. The agreement has been regularly renewed since then. Their bargain has been kept.

WOMEN AND EQUALITY

It is still not common to find many women active in affairs beyond the realm of family. In fact, women were not allowed to vote on a national level until 1971. Earlier, voting had been restricted to what was constitutionally called "a circle of free men," which specifically excluded women. They could not vote in Glarus canton elections until 1972. In 1973, they finally could vote in Obwalden and Nidwalden. The women in Appenzell are still waiting for that basic privilege.

Left: A policewoman directing traffic   Right: Opera star Lisa Della Casa

Despite the political restrictions, whether overt or under the surface, more and more young women are looking for job opportunities. About one out of three women now work outside the home. It is not rare to find female cab drivers or even Protestant ministers, at least in the larger urban areas. As they become economically independent, women are consequently demanding more voice in governmental affairs and more cultural and schooling opportunities.

The struggle for equality remains an uphill fight in this male-dominated society. As early as 1968, Lise Girardin became the first woman to serve as a mayor of a Swiss city—Genève. In 1984, Elisabeth Kopp, a lawyer from Zürich, was the first woman ever elected to the seven-person Federal Council, the chief executive governing body in Switzerland.

Other Swiss women have made important contributions to the world. Professor Heidi Fritz-Niggli was an internationally known mineralogist. Verena Meyer specialized in atomic energy studies. Opera stars Lisa Della Casa and Maria Stader have performed all over the world, as has actress Maria Schell.

THE SWISS ARMY

There is one job that is almost strictly reserved for the men: every able-bodied male must serve in the Swiss army. This is an important cornerstone of Switzerland's freedom. The country's citizen army is ready at all times, as a sort of national guard.

After training at the School of Recruits, a solider is free to go back home with his uniform and weapon. Every year, he attends three weeks of maneuvers. The enlisted man stays ready for service from age twenty until fifty. Officers are on call until the age of fifty-five.

The idea behind this "nation under arms" is to show any potential enemy that Switzerland is always ready to defend itself. The Swiss won't go out of their way to make trouble. But they will defend their rights.

Swiss of all ages know it is necessary to do their duty. Serving in the military is a very important civic responsibility, as is voting. Nobody seems to question the need for such an institution.

EDUCATION

A national educational policy has been hard to put into effect in Switzerland because education is under the control of each canton instead of being centralized at the federal level. Each school system is therefore different, based on the individual canton's traditions and customs.

School is compulsory and free, lasting from seven to nine years, depending on the canton. All the cantons offer programs for physically and mentally handicapped youngsters, as well as meals, services of doctors and psychologists, and transportation when needed.

Eating breakfast before school

Children begin their education in a preschool nursery before moving on to a primary level when they are six or seven. At the end of the required period, the older pupils can leave school to work. This may vary from canton to canton. Most, however, go on to a "nonvocational continuation school." Attendance at these upper-level institutions ranges from one to four years. Instead of classroom study and homework, the courses usually involve a hands-on apprenticeship in a job or on a farm. Some pupils go on to the lower secondary school, which offers more extensive business and traditional courses.

If a pupil finally passes an all-important final examination, he or she can move up to a more advanced technical school or to a university. The test is very hard and requires a great deal of study. It could include questions in Latin and Greek, modern languages such as English, science and mathematics, and business studies, depending on the type of education that the pupil has received. Test results will often determine what career options are available.

*The Conservatory
of Music in Bern*

For more training in a specific subject, there are specialized schools for occupations such as violin makers, cheese makers, hotel staff, and other service occupations. In those institutions, the students learn from master craft workers and experienced professionals.

Switzerland has eight universities: in St. Gallen, Basel, Bern, Fribourg, Genève, Lausanne, Neuchâtel, and Zürich. There are also federal institutes of technology at Lausanne and Zürich. About thirty thousand students are enrolled at the university level; probably one in five is a foreigner.

There are five hundred private schools in Switzerland, most represented by the Federation of Swiss Private Schools. Some eighty thousand young people attend these institutions scattered about the country. Genève, headquarters for many international corporations and site of some of the United Nations' European offices, has the largest concentration of private schools. The International School of Genève, which was established in 1924 by the League of Nations, serves young people of more than ninety nationalities. Its three campuses accommodate 2,600 enrollees from kindergarten through secondary school.

Even adults can return for more schooling. Educational institutions, private businesses, and social clubs offer courses ranging from computer programming to traditional folk art and furniture painting. Most classrooms are packed for the length of the course work. Love of learning seems to be ingrained in the Swiss, no matter what their age.

STANDARD OF LIVING

The standard of living in Switzerland, at least for a Swiss national, is relatively high. People have the sampling of material goods that mark a twentieth-century industrial society: washing machines, television sets, electric can openers, and other conveniences.

But land is expensive and building costs can soar beyond the reach of working-class Swiss. Therefore, most people live in furnished apartments. Long blocks of towering concrete flats reach out like tentacles in all directions from the cities. While many of the apartment balconies are gaily draped with overflowing flower boxes, these modern buildings still lack the outside charm found in older Swiss neighborhoods.

Luckily, most towns have retained their quaint central districts, with cobblestone side streets and gingerbread buildings that date back centuries. However, these same inner cities are suffering from depopulation as younger, more affluent Swiss seek up-to-date lodgings farther out from town.

Houses along the Aare River (left) in Thun and modern apartments (right) in Zürich

The Swiss remain basically an urban people. Barely 7 percent of the population are still farmers; four fifths live in towns of more than five thousand persons, generally in the plateau cantons.

Consequently, the demand for living space around the cities is constantly increasing, just as high meadows and Alpine farms are abandoned to encroaching scrub brush. Swiss social scientists fear that rural flight is adding more pressure to what they see as overpopulated urban regions. More people live in the central lowlands than in The Netherlands. The density of residents in Zürich is greater than anywhere in Japan, considered one of the most populated nations on earth. Scientists urge developers to be more cautious with their building projects, fearing the effect on the land and people by a growing blot of concrete and asphalt. Planned land use is considered one of this landlocked country's most pressing environmental concerns.

Old-age insurance, financed by worker contributions, provides rent allowances and annuities to men over 65 and women over 62 and helps widows, orphans, and invalids.

SOCIAL SERVICES

Another prime consideration of the Swiss is care of the elderly. Due to a falling birth rate, there are fewer active people being taxed to provide for the rise in services needed for the older citizens. Social security in Switzerland is both a federal and a cantonal responsibility. There is a compulsory federal old-age and survivors' insurance plan, which is expected to fill in the economic gap if a family's major breadwinner dies.

In addition, employers take out individual insurance plans for their workers. Private life insurance and bank savings form a "third leg" of economic protection for retired citizens. The Swiss are probably the most insured people in the world.

Medical services are considered above average. There are both private and canton-owned hospitals.

The extensive range of services available to the Swiss gives the small, landlocked country the best of many worlds. It is a modern industrial state, even without huge deposits of natural resources. Yet its literate and highly educated people, with characteristic vigor, assure that tasks will be quickly and precisely accomplished. Problems are overcome in the same way. After all, that's how the Swiss have been doing it for centuries.

Chapter 8

LAND OF KIDS AND SCHWINGEN

Switzerland's people are hardy products of their land. "In Swiss nature lies our destiny," a Swiss philosopher once wrote.

The ascent to summer pastures in the Alps is an important yearly event for Swiss mountain folk. A flower-bedecked procession of cattle winding up the trails is led by the "queen cow," from whose neck hangs a huge bell. Herdsmen follow, their carts packed with utensils for living an entire summer in the mountains. This custom keeps the people in tune with the harmonious seasonal changes, reminds them of their past, and emphasizes their dependence on the surroundings.

CELEBRATING CHILDREN

Each year several children's festivals are held throughout German and French Switzerland to celebrate the beginning of summer. The largest events include the *Solennitat* in Burgdorf, the *Rutenzug* in Brugg, the *Maienzug* in Aarau, and the youth festivals in Lenzburg and Zofingen. There are also end-of-spring parades for youngsters in Neuchâtel, Lausanne, and Genève.

Schoolgirls dress in their fluffiest white dresses, and boys wear starched shirts and Sunday pants. There is usually a morning church service, followed by games and dancing in the central parks of each city.

The St. Gallen Children's Festival is the best known of them all. The event, which began in 1824, is held every two years simply to honor children. Up to ten thousand youngsters parade through the streets, waving to their friends and proud families lining the route.

CHILDREN'S LITERATURE

Love of youngsters is ingrained in the Swiss mentality. The tale about William Tell and his son is one of the world's best-known stories. Other examples in Swiss folklore show how the traditional Swiss view of society focuses on the interrelationship of the entire family, not just on adults. This is demonstrated in the classic story *Heidi*, written in 1880 by Johanna Spyri. Heidi is an orphan who journeys to an Alpine village to live with her grandfather. Spyri's delightful account traces Heidi's adventures as she copes with growing up.

The full title of the book shows Swiss insight and inbred feeling toward youngsters: *Heidi, Her Years of Wandering and Learning, A Story for Children and Those Who Love Children.* *Heidi* has now been printed in braille and in thirty languages, including Siamese and Icelandic.

Perhaps the most famous Swiss writer was Johann David Wyss, who, in 1813, wrote *The Swiss Family Robinson.* That book described the rollicking adventures of a shipwrecked family whose quick thinking got them out of many scrapes. Multi-talented Wyss also wrote the lyrics for an early version of the Swiss national anthem as well as collected Swiss folktales.

Left: *A statue depicting Heidi in Maienfeld*
Right: *Carved dollhouses*

OTHER ARTS FOR CHILDREN

The love of youngsters extends into other artistic fields. In the early 1900s, Emile Jaques-Dalcroze composed lilting children's songs that are still sung in schools and on playgrounds throughout Switzerland. The popular nineteenth-century artist Albert Anker painted intricate scenes from his childhood days. Otto Meyer-Amden grew up in a Bern orphanage and, as an adult, used memories of his youth there as the basis for some paintings. Today, Hans Fischer and Alois Carigiet are renowned illustrators of children's books.

ART AND CRAFTS

Swiss artists have always been leaders in the European cultural scene. A dedicated Society of Swiss Painters was formed in 1866 to promote the works of its members. One of its primary goals was encouraging the government to help support the art world. Many famous painters are Swiss, including Ferdinand Hodler, Cuno

101

Above: A wood carver and his bears
Right: One of Paul Klee's whimsical paintings

Amiet, and Louis Soutter. Soutter also played first violin in the Orchestre de la Suisse Romande of Genève. Another famous artist with a dual career was Charles-Edouard Jeanneret, who was world famous as an architect under his nickname of Le Corbusier.

Early Swiss folk art, whether furniture painting or embroidery, remains a riot of vibrant design. Drawing on their experiences with nature, the craft workers used flowers, animals, and landscapes for their inspiration. Painters Peter Stampfli and Alfred Hofkunst currently are producing beautiful pieces of art in various mediums.

Painter and graphic artist Paul Klee is especially remembered for his charming, usually humorous paintings with delicate lines and colors. Alberto Giacometti is known for his lean, metal sculptures.

Art museums and private galleries in Bern, Basel, Genève, and Zürich are famous for collections of old masters and newly discovered artists. Even the smaller towns are proud of their local museums. The Swiss have always considered themselves patrons of the arts. The opening of a show will bring out hundreds of viewers who are quick to praise or critique.

Two contemporary painters are becoming well known for their expressionism. Martin Disler is a master of oils and often uses a colored wash on paper. Young Peter Kunz-Opsersi specializes in graphite drawings and mixed media for his mythological presentations, which are influenced by the ideas of Swiss psychologist Carl Gustav Jung. There is often such cross-fertilization of talent in Swiss creativity.

Even Swiss advertising art is known for its inventiveness, treating many themes in a light-hearted manner that quickly grabs attention. International clients flock to the nation's graphics studios, seeking bold, bright promotional materials for their services or industrial goods.

MUSIC

Music is another Swiss passion. The Orchestre de la Suisse Romande of Genève is world famous and so is its founder and first conductor, Ernest Ansermet. Concerts and music festivals—from classical to jazz—are held in shaded parks, vast halls, and on roped-off street corners. Recent Swiss composers are noted for their talented linking of German, French, and Italian musical styles, a carryover from their multiethnic makeup. Frank Martin, Arthur Honegger, and Willy Burkhard are among the best-known composers.

Development of modern Swiss music owes a great deal to the Basel Academy of Music. Under strict discipline, young people are encouraged to try new forms and styles. Highly respected teachers at the academy attract students from around the world. From the academy, polished musicians have joined orchestras around the world.

Musicians playing at a village festival

Folk music is still popular in Switzerland. Many villages have bands consisting of a violin, cello, bass violin, and a "hackbrett," which is similar to a dulcimer. In the folk music of central Switzerland, the clarinet is used. Sometimes in Valais and the Grisons, trumpets and trombones are added.

The fife and drum associations of Basel and Valais promote their own brand of traditional thumping, bumping Swiss "soul music" at festival time. The Basel *Fasnacht*, or Basel Carnival, is one of the most exciting folk fests in Switzerland. Wearing elaborately carved wooden masks and beribboned costumes reminiscent of legendary goblins and beasts, members of carnival associations called *cliques* parade with lanterns and torches through the darkened city. Rattling drumrolls reverberate from the old, chipped stone walls. Shrill fifes add birdlike counterpoint to the quick-stepping beat. *Fasnacht* is usually held prior to Lent to mark the approaching death of winter. In addition, the silly antics of the marchers make fun of human frailties.

Left: A jazz festival at Neuchâtel   Right: Philosopher and writer Jean-Jacques Rousseau

On a more modern front, jazz has found a friendly home and a receptive audience in Switzerland with such groups as the Tremble Kids and the Darktown Strutters. The usually staid director of finance for Basel performed for a time with the Strutters. The Montreux Jazz Festival is very popular.

LITERATURE

The Swiss are bold creators. Their thinkers have helped change how the world looks at itself.

Jean-Jacques Rousseau, the son of a watchmaker, was a Swiss-French philosopher of the eighteenth century who wrote impressive intellectual essays. Rousseau's ideas of liberty and the equality of man were accepted by the French revolutionaries and still influence many scholars today.

Psychologist Carl Gustav Jung proposed theories that helped people get in touch with their hearts and spirits. Karl Barth was one of Protestantism's most prominent theologians. He emphasized the necessity of faith in relationships with God.

Charles-Ferdinand Ramuz, a poet and novelist, is one of the most prominent twentieth-century writers. He collaborated with Igor Stravinsky in writing "Histoire du Soldat." Jeremias Gotthelf (born Albert Bitzius) depicted village life, and Francisco Chiesa wrote about his native Ticino. Gottfried Keller wrote in German, while Pieder Lansel used the Romansh language. Max Frisch and Friedrich Dürrenmatt are known for their novels and plays.

COMMUNICATION

Swiss newspapers are often affiliated with a political party, giving them an influence that is much stronger than their circulation shows. The largest daily newspaper is *Der Blick* of Zürich. Other major Swiss papers are the *Neue Züricher Zeitung* (Zürich) and the *Journal de Genève*.

Illustrated weekly and monthly magazines are popular. There are many specialized publications with large readerships, such as the magazine of the Touring Club Suisse. French and German radio and television magazines sell thousands of copies, featuring program listings and stories about stars and shows.

There are few Swiss-made feature films; however, producers such as Henry Brandt make excellent documentaries. One of Brandt's best known works is *When We Were Children*. Claude Goretta's astute observations of human behavior in *The Invitation* earned him a major prize in the 1973 Cannes Film Festival, a prestigious international film contest. The latest American, British, German, Italian, and French movies are shown in Swiss theaters.

Television and radio is under the direction of the Swiss

German   French   Italian   Romansh

Areas where the four major
languages are spoken

Many items are available from this newsstand

Broadcasting Company, a public firm established in 1931 and operating under federal authority. Viewers can choose from six or more television channels, some of which offer shows from outside the country. Each of Switzerland's languages is represented in the programming.

Broadcast transmitters and lines are maintained by the post office, an umbrella organization that also operates the country's bus routes and handles telephone and telegraph communications.

FOOD

Cooking is another form of Swiss art, drawing from all the country's ethnic traditions. One of the famous dishes of Switzerland is fondue. Hungry eaters skewer bits of bread, meat, vegetables, or even cake and dunk them into melted cheese, hot oils, chocolate, or other sauces.

Tourists enjoying cheese fondue (left) and a display of basler leckerli *(right), a gingerbread specialty*

In the western lake districts, fish is a base for many meals. A Swiss menu might contain *friture de perchettes,* fillets of lake perch fried in butter, or *croûtes aux morilles,* mushrooms served on toast.

Swiss pastry is tempting. Sugar buns and spiced honey cakes can be dangerous for dieters. The *gugelhopf* is a huge bun with a hollow center stuffed with fresh whipped cream. *Birnbrot* is a fruitcake made with dried pears.

HOLIDAYS

December 6 is a day when children eat a great deal, then go to bed to await the arrival of St. Nicholas. Good children get oranges, apples, and nuts. The bad ones in Zürich are supposedly carried away in the saint's big sack and told to clean up after his donkey. (The Swiss Santa or *Samichlaus* doesn't use reinde r.)

Candies ar. 1 sweet cakes are brightly wrapped and placed under the Christmas tree. But before impatient youngsters get to gobble

At Christmas, special cookies are made (left)
and city streets are beautifully decorated (right)

the goodies, they must recite special Yule poems. In French-speaking cantons, however, the young revelers usually have to wait until January 1 to open their gifts.

A more reserved celebration, Swiss National Day on August 1, is marked by orchestral concerts, speeches, and parades. The anniversary was first celebrated in 1891 to commemorate the pact made by the three original cantons in 1291. Family visits provide an excuse for picnics and special holiday meals. Celebrations conclude with nighttime fireworks and roaring bonfires high on the hills. From a distance, the fiery lights flicker like the eyes of Alpine monsters lost in the mountain darkness.

SPORTS

To encourage its own citizens to get out and see their country, the Swiss National Tourist Office recently announced a campaign promoting hiking. The tourist officials wanted the Swiss

Sailing boards on Silvaplana Lake and ice curling in Gstaad

themselves to experience more of what their country offers in the outdoors, as well as to savor the leg-stretching exercise. The program was a success.

Almost all hikers use a walking stick curved like a cane but with a sharp point on the bottom. This helps prevent slipping when scrambling up a steep slope. Metal souvenir badges decorate the sticks, indicating the places their owners have visited. An experienced stroller might have dozens of the tiny, multicolored plates nailed to his or her cane.

The Rhine River valley between Reichenau and the Grisons Oberland has excellent hiking opportunities and is the best way to see the Swiss countryside. Deep valleys slash the flanks of the cliffs as if a mythological sword tried to carve the rock. Vestiges of prehistoric landslides lie in crumpled heaps at the foot of jagged cliffs. Stone and wood farmhouses are scattered around the

Hikers can come across wonderful sights, like this little farm in the mountains.

patchwork fields and black-green stands of evergreens. The mountains poke white tips into the clouds. Hiking trails lead into Switzerland's secret corners, perhaps to a waterfall exploding over a cliff or to a ledge above the rollicking crimson coaches of the Glacier Express. Numerous vantage points overlook the railroad tracks that snake through the lower gorges.

The Swiss also like swimming, rowing, sailing, ice hockey, gymnastics, and bike racing. There are more than fifty sporting organizations in the country. One of the largest is the Swiss Association for Football (soccer) and Athletics, which has more than eighty thousand members.

The Swiss are among the best marksmen in the world, due to their military training. They always capture many trophies and ribbons at international shooting competitions.

Two sports are typically Swiss. *Hornussen* has features similar to

The city of Mürren has a balloon sport week.

golf, cricket, tennis, and baseball. The game is played by two teams, the "strikers" and the "killers." The strikers use long clubs to knock a disk called the *hornuss* (hornet) as far as possible down a marked field. With their own clubs, the killers try to hit the disk and prevent it from getting very far. If the hornet lands safely on the field, the killers lose a point. If they knock it down, they gain a point. The team with the most points wins.

Schwingen is Swiss wrestling. The combatants wear special trousers. The right hand of each man grabs the waistband and the left hand the leg band of his opponent. Each man attempts to lift the other and throw him down. Then he must hold the man's back to the ground. When a grunting fighter loses both handholds or when his shoulder blades touch the ground, he is defeated. The sweating victor usually gets a wreath of oak leaves as a prize.

Farms along the Grand Saint Bernard Pass

ENCHANTMENT OF SWITZERLAND

Switzerland is an enchanting nation, with an intricate mix of traditions and customs, political savvy, business sense, and brilliant culture. It has much to teach the rest of the world. Yet even Switzerland is more vulnerable than ever in this atomic age. The friendly mountains can no longer be considered the protective barriers they once were. However, neutral Switzerland steadfastly remains a calm refuge in a turbulent era when strife and violence are too-common headlines. It's no wonder that the leaders of such superpowers as the Soviet Union and the United States can find political breathing space in this tiny crossroads nation. Their much-heralded summit meeting in November of 1985 was only the latest in a centuries-long list of pilgrimages to this oasis of sense. Switzerland offers enemies the opportunity to air their distrust of each other, express their fears, and, maybe, reach common ground on their dreams.

MAP KEY

Aarau	B4	Ilanz	C5	Rolle	C2
Aare River	B3	Inn River	C5	Rorschach	B5
Ageri, Lake	B4	Interlaken	C3	Rüti	B4
Airolo	C4	Joux, Lake	C2	Ste. Croix	C2
Altdorf	C4	Jungfrau (mountain)	C3	St. Gallen	B5
Altstätten	B5	Kandersteg	C3	St. Gotthard Tunnel	C4
Andermatt	C4	Kreuzlingen	B5	St. Maurice	C3
Appenzell	B5	Kriens	B4	Samedan	C5
Arbon	B5	La Chaux-de-Fonds	B2	Sankt (Saint) Moritz	C5
Arosa	C5	La Locle	B2	Sargans	B5
Arth	B4	Langenthal	B3	Sarine River	C3
Baden	B4	Langnau in Emmental	C3	Sarnen	C4
Basel	B3	Lausanne	C2	Sarnen, Lake	C4
Bellinzona	C5	Lenk	C3	Schaffhausen	B4
Bern	C3	Les Haudères	C3	Schwyz	B4
Bernina Pass	C6	Liestal	B3	Scuol	C6
Biasca	C4	Linth River	B5	Sempacher Lake	B4
Biel	B3	Locarno	C4	Sierre	C3
Biel, Lake	B3	Lötschberg Tunnel	C3	Simplon Pass	C4
Birs River	B3	Lucerne, Lake	C4	Sion	C3
Bodensee		Lugano	C4	Solothurn	B3
(Lake Constance)	B5	Luzern	B4	Splügen	C5
Brienz, Lake	C3	Maggia River	C4	Splügen Pass	C5
Broye River	C2	Maloja Pass	C5	Stans	C4
Buchs	B5	Martigny-Ville	C3	Stockhorn (mountain)	C3
Bulle	C3	Matterhorn		Tendre (mountain)	C2
Burgdorf	B3	(mountain)	C3	Terrible (mountain)	B3
Carouge	C2	Meiringen	C4	Thalwil	B4
Cevio	C4	Mesocco	C5	Thun	C3
Chasseral (mountain)	B3	Monte Rosa		Thun, Lake	C3
Chur	C5	(mountain)	D3	Ticino River	C4
Cossonay	C2	Monthey	C2	Tödi (mountain)	C4
Davos	C5	Montreux	C2	Uster	B4
Delémont	B3	Morat, Lake	C3	Vallorbe	C2
Diablerets (mountain)	C3	Morges	C2	Versoix	C2
Einsiedeln	B4	Moudon	C2	Vevey	C2
Engelberg	C4	Nesslau	B5	Visp	C3
Erstfeld	C4	Neuchâtel	C2	Wädenswil	B4
Finsteraarhorn		Neuchâtel, Lake	C2	Wallen, Lake	B5
(mountain)	C4	Oberwald	C4	Wattwil	B5
Flawil	B5	Olivone	C4	Weisshorn	
Fleurier	C2	Olten	B3	(mountain)	C3
Frauenfeld	B4	Orsières	C3	Wettingen	B4
Fribourg	C3	Paglia (mountain)	C5	Wil	B5
Geneva, Lake	C2	Pilatus (mountain)	C4	Winterthur	B4
Genève	C2	Piz Kesch (mountain)	C5	Wolhusen	B4
Glärnisch (mountain)	C4	Pontresina	C5	Yverdon	C2
Glarus	B5	Porrentruy	B3	Zermatt	C3
Gr. Combin		Poschiavo	C6	Zernez	C6
(mountain)	D3	Rheinwaldhorn		Zug	B4
Grenchen	B3	(mountain)	C5	Zug, Lake	B4
Gstaad	C3	Rhine River	B4, C5	Zürich	B4
Hallwil Lake	B4	Rhône River	C3	Zürich Lake	B3
Herisau	B5	Rigi (mountain)	B4	Zweisimmen	C3

114

© Copyright by Rand McNally & Co. R.L. 86-S-44

FEDERAL REPUBLIC

BADEN-WÜRTTEMBERG

SWITZERLAND

ITALIA

MINI-FACTS AT A GLANCE

GENERAL INFORMATION

Official Names: Swiss Confederation; Schweizerische Eidgenossenschaft, in German; Confederation Suisse, in French; Confederazione Svizzera, in Italian; Confederaziun Helvetica, in Romansch

Official Languages: German (65 percent), French (18 percent), Italian (10 percent)

Government: The federal constitution of 1848, revised in 1874, converted what was previously a federation of states into a single federal state with a common post office, army, bicameral legislature, and judiciary, without any customs or commercial barriers. The federal constitution of 1874 established a strong central government while maintaining large powers of control in each canton. The basic unit of Swiss government is the commune, which is like a city with its own constitution and laws. Next comes the district, which is like a county. Both are under the supervision of the canton. Last comes the canton, which is similar to a state or province. Executive authority in the canton is vested in the state council and legislative authority is in the grand council.

Since January 1979 Switzerland has had twenty-three cantons. They are states which, like the nation itself, have their own constitutions, legislatures, executives, and judiciaries. They are incorporated in the confederation. The confederation has a two-chamber legislature — the Federal Assembly — consisting of the National Council and the Council of States. The two hundred seats in the National Council are distributed among the cantons according to the population; the Council of States has forty-six members, two from each canton. Executive power is in the hands of the Federal Council, consisting of seven members elected by a joint meeting of both chambers of the Federal Assembly for a four-year term. The federal president is chosen from among the members of the Federal Council and holds the office for a year while still running one of the departments.

The highest court is the federal tribunal; its twenty-six to thirty judges and twelve to fifteen alternates must be somewhat evenly divided among the three language groups.

The people can exert a significant degree of influence on national policy through the mechanisms of the referendum and the initiative. A referendum can be called by a petition with a minimum of thirty thousand signatures. For an initiative (proposal for legislation, which may include amending the constitution), 100,000 signatures are required. In some ways the Swiss government is one of the most democratic in the world. Women, however, have been able to vote only since 1971.

Flag: A white cross on a red ground; the arms of the cross are of equal length, each arm being one sixth longer than it is broad.

Coat of Arms: A white cross on a red shield

National Anthem: "Swiss Psalm"

Money: The basic unit is the franc. In 1986 the franc was worth around $0.50 in U.S. dollars.

Weights and Measures: Switzerland uses the metric system.

Population: 6,473,000, (1985 estimate; distribution, 60.4 percent urban, 39.6 percent rural); 1980 census, 6,365,960

Cities:

Zürich	369,522
Basel	182,143
Genève	165,505
Bern	145,254
Lausanne	63,278

(Population figures based on 1980 census)

GEOGRAPHY

Highest Point: Dufourspitze of Monte Rosa, 15,204 ft. (4,634 m). The highest permanently established settlement is the village of Juf at 6,975 ft. (2,126 m) in the Avers Valley in Grison.

Lowest Point: Shore of Lake Maggiore, 633 ft. (193 m) above sea level

Rivers: The main Swiss rivers—the Rhine, the Rhône, the Aare, the Reuss, the Inn, and the Ticino—rise in the St. Gotthard area.

River drainage: 67.7 percent of Swiss waters drain into the Atlantic (Rhine basin), 27.9 percent into the Mediterranean (Rhône basin), and 4.4 percent into the Black Sea (Inn basin).

Mountains: The Swiss Alps, in the south, are part of the largest mountain system in Europe. They cover about 60 percent of Switzerland but less than a fifth of the people live there. Snow blankets the region from three to five months a year. The unique panorama of the Swiss Alps is shaped by two dozen peaks over 13,124 ft. (4,000 m) high.
The Jura Mountains, in the northwest, consist of a series of parallel ridges separated by narrow valleys. Within Switzerland the highest mountain of the range is Mont Tendre, 5,518 ft. (1,682 m). The Jura Mountains are the home of the watch industry.

Climate: The climate varies widely from area to area because of the wide range of altitude. In general, temperature falls with increasing altitude. Yet there is a lower rate of decrease in winter, when the peaks are usually bathed in warm sunshine, and cold air and fogs often build up in the valley bottoms.

January temperatures average from 29 to 33° F. (-2 to 1° C) on the central plateau and in the mountain valleys. In summer the plateau is warm and sunny, but severe storms may occur. July temperatures on the plateau average from 65 to 70° F. (18 to 21° C). Many sheltered valleys sometimes become uncomfortably hot. In summer the higher slopes are cool or even cold. The canton of Ticino, which extends southward toward the Italian plains, has a Mediterranean climate with hot summers and mild winters. The central plateau receives from 40 to 45 in. (100 to 114 cm) of precipitation a year. Sheltered valleys usually have less. In some high areas yearly precipitation totals more than 100 in. (250 cm). A dry, warm southerly wind often blows into the Alpine valleys. It is called the *Föhn*.

Greatest Distances: East to west — 213 mi. (343 km)
North to south — 138 mi. (222 km)

Area: 15,942 sq. mi. (41,288 km²), including 523 sq. mi. (1,355 km²) of inland water

Plant Life: The plants of Switzerland are abundant and varied. Switzerland has areas belonging to every zone of plant life in Europe. The Alpine plant life is particularly notable for its variety of form and splendor of color: among the species are rhododendron, gentian, Alpine pansy, primula, globe flower, silver thistle, soldanella, Alpine aster, edelweiss, Alpine poppy, and glacier buttercup. Of Switzerland's more than 3,000 flowering plants and ferns, 160 are protected by law.

Animal Life: The animal life of Switzerland is similar to that of other central European countries. The stock of game includes reindeer, chamois, red deer, ibexes, and some recently established sika deer from Asia. Stocks of pheasants, hares, and partridges are released every year. Marmots are to be found all over the Alps. A number of species are protected by federal law. Regulations on shooting and fishing vary from canton to canton.

EVERYDAY LIFE

Food: The cuisine of the various parts of Switzerland is influenced by that of its neighboring countries. However, there are a number of specifically Swiss dishes that use locally produced ingredients from Switzerland's lakes and rivers. Fish dishes play a large part in the Swiss menu. Pike, trout, barbel, whitefish, dace, char, and perch are favorites. Blausee trout are considered a particular delicacy. Potatoes are eaten mainly in northern Switzerland, where the influence of Germany is felt. The Swiss are particularly good at making cakes and sweets; among the most tempting are *basler leckerli* (gingerbread), *zuger kirschtorte* (cream-filled meringues), and the *zabaglione* of Ticino. Switzerland has a rich assortment of excellent sausages. Swiss chocolate is known all over the world.

Housing: Swiss domestic buildings have a carefully cherished individuality of style with differences and contrasts not only between city and country but between different parts of the country. In Appenzell, where there is relatively high rainfall, the house and farm buildings are brought together under a single roof. The fronts of the houses, built of timber, are frequently broken by windows. In northeastern Switzerland the houses are mainly half-timbered with whitewashed panels between the framing. In the Jura there are massive stone-built structures, broad based with roofs that come down over the walls. In the Bernese Oberland, the "log cabin" method of construction is preferred. In the area of Lake Geneva, the rear of the house, with deep eaves, faces onto the street. In the Ticino the houses are similar to those found on the frontier in Italy, with walls and roofs of stone. Modern buildings in the larger cities use glass and steel.

Holidays:

January 1, New Year's Day
January 6, Epiphany
Good Friday, Easter, and Easter Monday
May 1, Labor Day
Ascension Thursday
Whit Monday
Corpus Christi (in cantons with predominately Catholic population)
August 1, National Day
August 15, Assumption Day
November 1, All Saints' Day
December 25-26, Christmas

Culture: Most Swiss literature has been written in German. The most famous classics are *Heidi* by Johanna Spyri and *The Swiss Family Robinson* by Johann David Wyss. Major nineteenth-century Swiss authors were Jeremias Gotthelf, who wrote simple but profoundly human stories of peasant life, and Gottfried Keller and Conrad Ferdinand Meyer, both of Zürich, who made an enduring contribution to literature in the German language. Carl Spitteler won the Nobel Prize in literature in 1919. Friedrich Dürrenmatt and Max Frisch are authors novels and plays that occupy a high place in contemporary German literature. Carl J. Burckhardt made an international contribution to the school of the Renaissance.

The history of Swiss culture is as varied and complex as the landscape of the country. This land of four languages has been open to influences from the wider world, and its art and architecture show affinities with those of the neighboring countries of Germany, Austria, France, and Italy.

The art movement called Dadaism was founded in Zürich in 1916. Outstanding Swiss artists of the twentieth century include the painter Paul Klee and the sculptors Alberto Giacometti and Jean Tinguely. Le Corbusier won fame in modern architecture.

Several Swiss cities have symphony orchestras, though the most famous is the Orchestre de la Suisse Romande of Genève, founded by Ernest Ansermet, and presently under the baton of Armin Jordan. Music lovers from all over come to an annual festival in Luzern and the Montreux Jazz Festival. Band music and folk dancing in local costumes are popular. Yodeling and playing the alpenhorn are popular activities. Lucarno hosts an annual international film festival.

Swiss folk art is still very much alive, and can be seen in painting, embroidery, wood carving, and hand weaving.

Sports and Recreation: Skiing is, of course, the most popular sport in Switzerland. But bobsledding, camping, and hiking in the mountains are also popular. Shooting matches are held frequently. Bicycling, boating, gymnastics, soccer, swimming, and wrestling are also common. Hornussen is a national game somewhat like baseball. One of the newest sports is hang gliding, which is taught in a number of schools. The most popular Swiss card game is jass, played with thirty-six cards in four suits.

Communication: Switzerland has more than 450 newspapers. More than half of the dailies are published in German, the others in French and Italian. The largest daily newspaper, *Der Blick* of Zürich, has a daily circulation of over 300,000. The government owns the three radio stations and three TV stations. Each broadcasts in one of the official languages. The government operates the postal, telegraph, and telephone systems.

Transportation: In spite of the mountains, Switzerland has a fine transportation system. The entire railroad network (3,150 mi. — 5,070 km) is owned by the government. There are many railroad tunnels through the Alps; the longest, the Simplon Tunnel, 12.3 mi. (19.8 km), is the longest in the world. There are over 30,000 mi. (48,000 km) of highways, but many mountain passes are closed during the winter. The St. Gotthard Road Tunnel (10.14 mi. — 16.32 km) is the longest highway tunnel in the world. The Rhine River connects Basel, Switzerland's only port, with the North Sea. Genève and Zürich have international airports. Swissair, Switzerland's airline, flies to about forty countries.

Education: In most cantons children are required to attend school from six through fourteen years of age. Instruction is in the local national language. There are three different kinds of high schools — those specializing in Greek or Latin; Latin and modern languages; and math and science. There are also vocational trade or technical schools. There are about 350 private boarding schools. Switzerland has eight universities. The oldest is the University of Basel, founded in 1460. The largest is the University of Zürich, with about ten thousand students. There are various other schools of higher learning, including two Federal Institutes of Technology, one in Zürich (where Albert Einstein studied and taught) and one in Lausanne.

Tourism: The income derived from tourism helps relieve the deficit in the balance of trade.

Defense: The purpose of the Swiss army is to preserve the independence of the country. Every male aged twenty to fifty is liable for military duty.

Health and Social Welfare: Health conditions in Switzerland are generally excellent, with a life expectancy at birth of 72.7 years for males and 79.6 for females (1981-82).

Principal Products:
Agriculture: milk, cheese
Manufacturing: Chemicals, pharmaceuticals, watches, leather, machinery, man-made fabrics, embroidery, silk, and textiles
Finance: Switzerland is a leading world banking center. The stability of the currency brings funds from many quarters.

IMPORTANT DATES

500 B.C.—Helvetii (a band of Celts) are living in Switzerland

15 B.C.—Roman occupation

1000s—Switzerland becomes part of the Holy Roman Empire

1291—Cantons of Uri, Schwyz, and Unterwalden form a confederation

1332-53—Confederation is enlarged by the admission of Luzern, Zürich, Glarus, Zug, and Bern

1394—Austria renounces its claims to sovereignty over the forest cantons of Luzern, Glarus, and Zug

1439—Confederation breaks free of the Hapsburg empire

1460—University of Basel founded

1476-77—Burgundian War; confederation fights against Charles the Bold

1481—Fribourg and Solothurn join the confederation

1501—Basel and Schaffhausen join the confederation

1505—The Swiss Guard founded

1513—Appenzell admitted to the confederation

1679—Daniel Jean Richard makes the first Swiss clock

1798—France occupies the whole of Switzerland, dissolves the old confederation and establishes the Helvetian Republic

1803—St. Gallen, Aargau, Thurgau, Ticino, and Vaud join the confederation

1815—Valais, Neuchâtel, and Genève join the confederation; Switzerland declares policy of neutrality

1844—The first train arrives in Switzerland

1848—A new federal constitution is adopted

1863—The Red Cross is founded

1865—The Matterhorn is conquered

1870—Switzerland remains neutral in the Franco-Prussian War

1874—Federal constitution is revised; federal government is assigned responsibility for foreign policy, the army, economic affairs, and partial responsibility for justice

1914-18—Switzerland maintains its neutrality during World War I

1920—First meeting of the League of Nations held in Genève

1938-45—Switzerland remains neutral during World War II

1948—Switzerland becomes a member of UNESCO

1959—Switzerland joins European Free Trade Association

1971—Women granted right to vote

1972—Switzerland joins European Community

1979—Jura becomes a Swiss canton

1981—Equal Rights Amendment passed

1986—Swiss voters reject their country's entry into United Nations; poison spilled from Sandoz warehouse kills all aquatic life for 180 mile stretch of Rhine River

IMPORTANT PEOPLE

Ernest Ansermet (1883-1969), musician and founder of the Orchestre de la Suisse Romande, its conductor from 1918 to 1966

Karl Barth (1886-1968), Protestant Reformed theologian and educator

Jakob Bernoulli (1654-1705), mathematician and physician, specialist in integral and differential calculus

Jakob Burckhardt (1818-97), art historian, pioneer in the history of culture

Jean Calvin (1509-64), French theologian and reformer who was banished from Paris in 1533 and took refuge in Basel; his academy founded in Genève in 1559 served as focal point for defense of Protestantism throughout Europe

Jean-Henri Dunant (1828-1910), philanthropist and founder of the Red Cross

Friedrich Dürrenmatt (1921-   ), author of novels and plays that occupy a high place in contemporary German literature

Leonhard Euler (1707-83), mathematician and physicist; one of the founders of the science of pure mathematics; author of works on analytic math, algebra, and other mathematical subjects

Max Frisch (1911-   ), playwright and novelist

Alberto Giacometti (1901-66), sculptor, known for elongated sculptures of solitary figures

Jeremias Gotthelf (1797-1854), born Albert Bitzius, author who depicted village life in Switzerland

Hermann Hesse (1877-1962), German author who emigrated to Switzerland in 1919; received Nobel Prize in literature in 1946

Ferdinand Hodler (1853-1918), painter

Arthur Honegger (1892-1955), Swiss-born French composer

Carl Gustav Jung (1875-1961), psychologist and psychiatrist; developer of analytic psychology

Gottfried Keller (1819-90), German-language lyric and epic poet and novelist

Paul Klee (1879-1940), modernist painter and pictorial artist; cofounder of the German asbtract school Blaue Reiter (1911); developed an individual style expressing the subconscious mind and fantasy in art

Emil T. Kocher (1841-1917), surgeon and professor, known especially for work on the thyroid gland and on osteomyelitis; winner of the Nobel Prize in physiology and medicine, 1909

Le Corbusier (1887-1965), pseudonym of Charles-Edouard Jeanneret; architect, painter, and writer; his works include a design for the Palace of the League of Nations in Genève; established a new style of housing that went beyond the normal functions of a house

Frank Martin (1890-1974), musician, best known in the U.S. for his "Petite Symphonic Concertante"

Paul H. Muller (1890-1965), chemist, discovered properties of DDT; received Nobel Prize in physiology or medicine in 1948

Henri Nestlé (1814-90), established chocolate manufacturing concern in 1867

Philippus A. Paracelsus (Paracelsus) (1493?-1541), alchemist and physician; taught that diseases are specific entities that can be cured by specific remedies; founder of modern science of medicine

Johann Heinrich Pestalozzi (1746-1827), educational reformer; emphasized concrete approach in education with objects used to develop powers of observation and reasoning; strongly influenced methods of instruction in Europe and America

Jean Piaget (1896-1980), psychologist, philosopher, and biologist who established a model for the psychological and intellectual development of children

Auguste Piccard (1884-1962), physicist; investigated radioactivity and atmospheric electricity; made balloon ascent of over 55,000 ft. (16,764 m) in Zürich, 1932

Charles Ferdinand Ramuz (1878-1947), spent eleven years in Paris before returning to his native canton of Vaud to write poetry, novels, and short stories inspired by his land and his people

Jean-Jacques Rousseau (1712-78), French philosopher and author born in Genève who anticipated many of the insights of modern social psychology

Leopold Ruzicka (1887-1976), chemist

Johanna Spyri (1827-1901), writer of children's books, known especially for *Heidi*

Marie Tussaud (1760-1850), modeler in wax; founder of Madame Tussaud's exhibition in London

Felix Valloton (1865-1925), painter and engraver

Alfred Werner (1866-1919), chemist; recipient of Nobel Prize in 1913

Ulrich Zwingli (1484-1531), religious reformer

INDEX

Page numbers that appear in boldface type indicate illustrations

About the Author

Martin Hintz lives with his family in Milwaukee, Wisconsin, and has visited Switzerland several times in his capacity as a travel writer. Hintz has skied in the Engadine Valley, walked the streets of St. Gallen, motored over the high Alps, photographed the Matterhorn, traveled in midwinter on the Glacier Express, and munched on ursenkase, a cheese from the Bernese Oberland. "It's an ongoing love affair," he says.

For helping to prepare Enchantment of the World: Switzerland, the author wishes to thank the directors and personnel of the Consulate General of Switzerland, the Swiss National Tourist Office (especially Walter Bruderer), the Embassy of Switzerland, Swissair, the Swiss Federal Railways, the Swiss Cheese Association, and the Pro Helvetia press service. Special mention should also go to the author's many Swiss friends and contacts including Karl Bosshard, Hans Sauser, Franco Moro, Roger Ballou, Emil Cadalbert, Max Keller, Hans P. Danuser, Dominik Gasser, Ruedi Mettler, Stefan F. Zehnder, Jürg and Denise Hochstrausse-Tenger, Raoul T. De Gendre, Liliane Conti, Sepp Josef Steiger, Jürg Dossegger, and the dozens of others who have been so helpful, such as master watch repairman Ralph Voelker, David Robinson of the Marlborough Gallery, and authors Neil Alexander and Sidney Clark.

P9-DEW-722

More I Like to Read® Books
by Emily Arnold McCully

3, 2, 1, Go!

"This succeeds both as entertainment and instruction; the pachyderms'
social interactions and STEM content are a delightful bonus."
—*Booklist*

★ "A sure hit."
—*Kirkus Review* (starred review)

Pete Likes Bunny

"A sympathetic take on a seldom-discussed situation."
—*Kirkus Reviews*

Pete Makes a Mistake

"This spot-on title is perfect for brand new readers."
—*School Library Journal*

Pete Won't Eat

★ "New readers will eat this up."
—*Kirkus Reviews* (starred review)

★ "The illustrations are priceless."
—*School Library Journal* (starred review)

Min Makes a Machine

Emily Arnold McCully

I Like to Read®

HOLIDAY HOUSE • NEW YORK

I Like to Read® books, created by award-winning
picture book artists as well as talented newcomers,
instill confidence and the joy of reading in new readers.

We want to hear every new reader say, "I like to read!"

_____

Visit our website for flash cards, activities, and more about the series:
www.holidayhouse.com/ILiketoRead
#ILTR
This book has been tested by an educational expert
and determined to be a guided reading level E.

I LIKE TO READ is a registered trademark of Holiday House Publishing, Inc.

Copyright © 2018 by Emily Arnold McCully
All Rights Reserved
HOLIDAY HOUSE is registered in the U.S. Patent and Trademark Office.
Printed and bound in December 2017 at Tien Wah Press, Johor Bahru, Johor, Malaysia.
The artwork was created with pen and ink and watercolor.
www.holidayhouse.com
First Edition
1 3 5 7 9 10 8 6 4 2

Library of Congress Cataloging-in-Publication Data is available.

ISBN 978-0-8234-3970-6 (hardcover)
ISBN 978-0-8234-3971-3 (paperback)

To all problem-solving girls

"Let's play!" called Min.
"Too hot," said Bess.
"Play with somebody else."

"I will make a fan," said Min.

"It's still too hot," said Ann.
"I wish we could swim."

"There is the old pool," said Ann.
"But it has no water," said Bess.

"I will look for water!" said Min.
"I am going home," said Ann.
"This is no fun."

"Look!" called Min.
"I found an old well."

"The water is at the bottom,"
said Bess.

"I will get it out,"
said Min.
Off she went.

Min came back.

She had a long tube.

Next she got
a hose.

Min put glue
on the tube.

Then she put the hose
on the tube.

"We are ready," said Min.
"How?" asked Bess.

Min put the tube
into the well.

"This is the hard part," said Min.

Min turned the tube . . .

and turned . . .

and turned . . .

and turned!

Water came out!

The pool filled up.

Bess and Min got in.

Ann jumped in too.

Splash!